GQ

DRINKS

DRINKS

FOREWORD BY
SALVATORE
CALABRESE

GQ

THE COCKTAIL
COLLECTION
FOR DISCERNING
DRINKERS

EDITED BY
PAUL HENDERSON

PHOTOGRAPHY BY
ROMAS FOORD

Contents

Foreword
Salvatore Calabrese

Modern men understand mixology. They get it, finally! I have been making cocktails since I was 12, but when I moved to the UK from Italy in the 1980s, I found cocktails were reserved either for fine hotel bars or for big nights out when you would be served large, lurid-coloured drinks with silly names – and probably a cocktail umbrella or two.

Today, men are just as likely to know their way around a Martini, a Manhattan and a Negroni as to be familiar with the beer choice at their local bar or the wine aisle at the supermarket. Cocktails have become part of our normal drinking repertoire.

It has not been an easy path. The 1970s and '80s are now seen as the dark ages in cocktail circles and it was hard to escape their clutches in the '90s. But as the foodie revolution took hold, so the world of drinks has caught up. Men understand when to drink a Martini and how to make an Old Fashioned. They know that a Daiquiri is not just something served super-sweet with mashed-up strawberries in it, but a fine drink with heritage. And that being seen with a Sazerac is just as masculine as having a pint of beer in your hand, maybe even more so!

From the mid-2000s, we entered a new golden age of cocktails. Young cocktail bartenders began to recognize that they were the heirs to that last great golden age, Prohibition, and to a line of even older drinks pioneers stretching back to the mid-1800s. The public began to see cocktail-making as a craft and a worthy profession again, just like in the old days.

Drinking and making cocktails says something about you. It says you are aware of the revolution that has taken place, that you care about ingredients, and that you know that not every vodka, whisky or brandy is made in the same way or tastes the same. With cocktails there is real heritage behind the classics, and to many people that is far more interesting than simply opening the screw-cap of a bottle of wine or popping the cap on a beer.

Go to a good bar in London, New York, Sydney or Singapore, and you will find a new generation of super-creative mixologists (no longer a dirty word) who will be happy to talk you through their homemade bitters, their house-infused bacon-flavoured bourbon or the botanicals used in their range of gins. But, more importantly, they can also knock out the core of our craft, the classics, making you a finely balanced Margarita, a nuanced Bloody Mary or a bracing julep. It should be easy for most men to include a few good cocktail bars among their list of favourite hang-outs.

At home, too, things have changed. Gone are the optics, the vermouth that sat in the cupboard for years, the lone bottle of Angostura bitters and the eight cubes of ice to be shared by everyone at a cocktail party. Today, if I am offered a G&T in someone's home, I am more likely to be given a choice of gins and a premium tonic water, and it will be served long, with lots of ice and a good squeeze of fresh lime.

If you are in the midst of creating your own home bar, a *GQ* man should have good-quality examples of whisky, gin, brandy, vodka, tequila and rum. You should keep your vermouth and your sherry (which is no longer just for your great-aunt) in the refrigerator and discard them after a few weeks once they have been opened. You should have fresh fruit available, as well as liqueurs that are not chock-full of artificial flavours, and feel confident to experiment with a range of different bitters, not just Angostura. You will have bags and bags of ice at your disposal, the required equipment and the right glassware. And you should know how to shake, stir and throw properly.

Who have we got to thank for all this? Mostly it is a result of the growing sophistication of our palates and the hard work of a generation of passionate bartenders, resulting in consumers thirsty for cocktails, places to drink them and the ability to make them. You only have to look at the popularity of vintage cocktails – that is, drinks made with the ingredients available at the time when they were originally created. I specialize in them at my bar at Playboy Club, London.

And, perhaps more than anything else, I know we are in a new era, because cocktail umbrellas are back in vogue again, only this time they're ironic.

Salute!

Frank Sinatra:
'Let me fix you a Martini
that's pure magic.'

Dean Martin:
'It may not make life's
problems disappear, but it'll
certainly reduce their size.'

Recipes by Ladislav Piljar

The Red Bar at Bam-Bou, London

Gin
by Amy Matthews

Held responsible for Hogarthian scenes of debauchery in the 18th century, for a decline in the afternoon productivity of Manhattan ad executives in the 1960s and, more recently, for inspiring hipsters in waistcoats to create drinks with names like Mr Fothergill's Most Peculiarly Splendid Libation, gin has rarely had a good press. So much more complex than vodka, it is, however, the backbone of a bartender's most dependable beverages: the reviving gin and tonic, or G&T, the invigorating Negroni and the most fundamental cocktail of all, the Martini. Some say gin's effect tends towards the morose, others cannot imagine a celebratory evening without it. However many characterful variations and myriad disguises gin inhabits, one thing is certain: it remains unequivocally the choice of the serious drinker.

Under its legal definition, gin is a clear, un-aged spirit made by two rounds of distillation – the first to produce the base spirit from wheat or maize, the second to flavour the spirit with selected botanicals, the most prominent of which must be juniper. Other flavours are entirely at the discretion of the distiller, but popularly include citrus peel, coriander and angelica root. Some gins have of course become notable for the addition of key flavours such as the cucumber and rose of Hendrick's, or the refreshing mix of grapefruit, orange and lime of a Tanqueray No. TEN.

Carrying with it a whiff of colonial times past, the G&T has gained a place and status in English life comparable to a cup of tea: refreshing yet comforting, simultaneously relaxing and invigorating. Its very character seems appropriately English: belying its clear, restrained appearance, gin has a no-nonsense approach to flavour and effect.

But the roots of gin itself are continental. Back in the 14th century, potions flavoured with juniper were used in Italy to guard against the Black Death. These juniper elixirs followed the disease across mainland Europe to Holland where they took root in the Netherlands, resulting in a profusion of genevers, early versions of a juniper-based spirit. By the end of the 17th century, the drink had made its way to England where it gained its English name, 'gin', and began to flourish in popularity leading to the enthusiastic and ruinous excesses of the next 50 years.

The Gin Act of 1751 put paid to the high level of consumption, largely by limiting the production of the spirit to only a handful of licensed major distillers. This new group of producers included such famous names as Greenall's (founded in 1761) and Gordon's (founded in 1769), and went on to dominate the now significantly cowed British gin scene for over a century. After continued disapproval of its consumption in the 19th century, gin's easy synchronicity with the party crowd brought it back to popularity in the early 20th century. It flowed in the glasses of the Bright Young Things throughout the Roaring Twenties, became the choice spirit of renowned hardened drinkers like Ernest Hemingway and Winston Churchill, and remained ubiquitous in the Martinis and Gimlets of the suited Sixties cocktail parties and power lunches. Gin finally lost out to the more fashionable vodka from

Q&A with
Ladislav Piljar

How did you get into the business? My mum was a pharmacist and I was always intrigued by that. Later, I started to realize how much these two professions have in common. We both help people, create different concoctions, listen to people over the counter and sell 'good drugs'! There was once a time when you could only get a drink in a drug store.

What is your bartending philosophy? I want my guests to leave happier and feeling better than when they first came in. Whatever happens, they have to have a good time. Always do things as best you can – until you find a better way of doing them.

Where can drinkers try your creations? At The Red Bar on the top floor of Bam-Bou restaurant, one of London's best-kept secrets.

Three great all-rounder gins recommended by Ladislav Piljar

1 Plymouth Navy Strength
2 Tanqueray No. TEN
3 Beefeater London Dry

the Seventies onwards, largely due to bombastic branding efforts that have since defined the spirits market in the UK. It has only recently regained its rightful place at the forefront of the cocktail and craft drinks movement, as well as the British drinks cabinet.

Sipsmith is an English company at the heart of this recent gin revival, kick starting a revival of small-batch, hand-crafted gins with its launch of the first copper distillery in London for almost 200 years. Fairfax Hall, director and co-founder, has seen the gin market change out of all recognition in the past few years: 'I believe this renaissance is founded on genuine credentials rather than passing fads. What it comes down to is the product: the one thing which runs through our whole ethos is uncompromising quality.' He sees no reason to worry that the market is reaching saturation, however, 'I think of gin in very much the same vein as good whisky: someone who loves whisky will have their go-to brand, but they'll also have a portfolio of other choices.'

Such is the explosion of distilleries in the last few years, there is now a gin for every occasion. And such is the UK's thirst for it, gin is imported from all over the world; new examples include the grape-spirits-based G'Vine from France and the maritime-influenced Gin Mare from Spain. In fact, it is really the Spanish who have owned the G&T for the last few years. Back when the English were still drinking single measures out of sad little glasses with a solitary slice of lemon in pubs, bars in Barcelona and Madrid were finding the real joy in the drink, serving generous doubles over a mountain of ice in a balloon glass to perfectly capture the aromas of the gin, the tonic and the garnish.

Today, England is finally feeling the change in drinking habits. Dav Eames, bar manager at London's acclaimed Gilbert Scott bar says: 'Customers are beginning to recognize the range of flavours, dimensions, styles and botanicals of gin. This spirit really is a new favourite among what was traditionally a vodka-drinking generation.' Across London in Soho, Graphic Bar is known for its offering of more than 180 different gins, something their bar manager James Huertas puts down to gin's flexibility and classic appeal. 'Gin has been used in cocktails for hundreds of years,' he explains. 'It's a malleable spirit that pairs with food and other flavours incredibly well. There is something for everyone when it comes to gin cocktails, from the Martini to the Clover Club.'

Whatever your preference, there has never been a better time to drink gin. Whether it's a handmade Martini from the silver trolley at Dukes in Mayfair, a dash of the current drinks cabinet favourite at home on a Friday evening or a pre-prandial sharpener at 33,000 feet, gin will continue through the decades of changing trends as a true classic. For the steadfast gin drinker, smugness has already proved its own reward, but an ice-cold G&T is the best prize of all.

The Hanky-Panky

The Hanky-Panky is believed to be the first truly famous cocktail to emerge from the legendary American Bar at The Savoy hotel. This concoction came to life in the early 1900s at the hands of Ada Coleman, the head bartender. Coleman invented the Hanky-Panky for Sir Charles Hawtrey, the premier comedy actor of his generation, who often came to see 'Coley' when he was in need of a drink with 'a bit of punch in it'. Upon being presented with Coley's first version of the Hanky-Panky, Hawtrey reportedly cried, 'By Jove! That is the real hanky-panky!' and the name stuck.

GLASSWARE
Sherry or Martini

ICE
Cubes to stir, none to serve

GARNISH
Orange twist

SERVES 1

½ **tsp** Fernet Branca
40ml (1¼fl oz) Beefeater gin
20ml (¾fl oz) Punt e Mes vermouth
20ml (¾fl oz) Cocchi Vermouth di Torino

Add the ingredients to a mixing glass with ice, starting with the Fernet Branca. Stir slowly and gently, then strain into a chilled sherry or Martini glass, being careful not to over-pour in order to maintain the fine balance of flavours in this drink. Garnish with an orange twist.

Bartender's Tip
The best way to make a lemon or orange twist is with a regular potato peeler. Use it just as you would on a potato for an easy, efficient twist.

Gin Punch à la Terrington

This drink originates from the second half of the 19th century, when making lemon sherbet was a popular way of preserving citrus juices. Gin punch is an excellent and refreshing summer drink, best enjoyed on one of those hot days when even lying in the shade seems like hard work. Lemon sherbet can be somewhat of a hassle to make, but I really recommend spending the little bit of extra time. It'll be worth it for this excellent gin punch.

GLASSWARE
Highball

ICE
Cubes to shake and to serve

GARNISH
Lemon wedge

SERVES 1

50ml (1¾fl oz) Tanqueray Dry gin
15ml (½fl oz) lemon sherbet (*see* below)
15ml (½fl oz) lemon juice
10ml (2 tsp) green Chartreuse
Soda water, to top up

For the lemon sherbet
(Makes 200ml/7fl oz)
Grated zest and juice of **3** lemons (you want **150ml/¼ pint** of juice)
150g (5oz) icing sugar

Bartender's Tip
A fun twist on Gin Punch à la Terrington is to try putting all the ingredients into a SodaStream. Then, when ready to serve, you only have to pour the drink over ice.

First make the lemon sherbet. Muddle together the lemon zest and icing sugar in a bowl until the mixture resembles a yellow paste. Add the lemon juice and stir into the lemon paste. Strain through a fine tea strainer and refrigerate until ready to use (it will last for up to 2 weeks).

To make the punch, add all the ingredients except the soda water to a shaker with ice. Shake, then pour into a highball glass over ice and top up with soda water to taste. Garnish with a lemon wedge.

Martinez

The true origin of the Martinez is murky at best: some say it was invented in San Francisco, while others maintain it comes from the nearby town of Martinez. Certain theories describe the Martinez as a variation of the classic Martini, while more say it's the other way around. Regardless, we know that the Martinez hails from the late 19th century in the midst of vermouth's rise to popularity with the bartenders of the age. The Martinez notably inverts the typical spirit/vermouth ratio of the Martini, providing a lighter, sweeter drink.

GLASSWARE
Coupette or Martini

ICE
None

GARNISH
Orange twist

SERVES 1

30ml (1fl oz) Bols Genever
  or Plymouth gin
60ml (2fl oz) Cocchi Vermouth
  di Torino
2 dashes of Angostura bitters

Add all the ingredients to a mixing glass. Stir well, then pour neat into a chilled coupette or Martini glass and garnish with an orange twist.

Bartender's Tip
This drink will always pair well with a savoury snack, such as Gentleman's Relish on toast, a hunk of mature Cheddar cheese or a Welsh rarebit.

White Lady

The White Lady became famous in the Twenties and has reappeared in different versions since. The most popular recipe (below) is from *The Savoy Cocktail Book*, a bartender's bible. There are two people who could possibly be the creators of the White Lady: Harry MacElhone from Ciro's Club in London and Harry Craddock, head bartender of the American Bar at The Savoy, London (and author of *The Savoy Cocktail Book*). What makes finding the truth difficult is that the two Harrys were great friends who often shared tips and recipes. Although we might never know the real story, we do know that it is one good drink.

GLASSWARE
Sherry or Martini

ICE
Cubes to shake, none to serve

GARNISH
Lemon twist

SERVES 1

50ml (1¾fl oz) Bombay Original gin
25ml (¾fl oz) lemon juice
25ml (¾fl oz) Cointreau
1 egg white

Add all the ingredients into a shaker with ice. Shake vigorously, then strain into a chilled Martini glass. Garnish with a lemon twist.

Bartender's Tip
My golden rule is always add egg white as the last ingredient to the shaker. If you mix egg white with gin by itself, the egg white will begin to 'cook' and harden, and the drink won't be as frothy as it needs to be.

The Bramble

The Bramble was created in 1984 by Dick Bradsell. Sometimes called 'the cocktail king', Bradsell was an innovative bartender whose simple, elegant drinks brought London's cocktail scene out of the age of overwrought gimmicks and into one of classic and refined cocktails. The Bramble is essentially a fancy gin sour, but the blackberry liqueur gives the drink enough individuality for it to remain as popular today as it was in 1984.

GLASSWARE
Highball or tumbler

ICE
Crushed

GARNISH
Lemon slice, raspberry or blackberry

SERVES 1

40ml (1¼fl oz) Tanqueray Dry gin
25ml (¾fl oz) lemon juice
15ml (½fl oz) sugar syrup
15ml (½fl oz) crème de mûre

Pour the gin, lemon juice and sugar syrup into a tumbler. Fill it to the top with crushed ice and stir gently. Pour the crème de mûre over the top and garnish with a lemon slice and a raspberry or blackberry.

Bartender's Tip
The Bramble comes in many different versions, but no matter which you choose, remember to keep a strong balance of sweet and sour, because that's the relationship that makes The Bramble so memorable.

The Pegu Club

The recipe for The Pegu Club cocktail was first published in *Barflies and Cocktails* by Harry MacElhone in 1927. Named after the gentleman's club in Burma (Myanmar), The Pegu Club was a taste of home for new settlers to the area. The cocktail fell out of favour following the British departure from Burma during World War II, but, after the opening of another Pegu Club in New York, it has experienced a resurgence in worldwide popularity.

GLASSWARE
Coupette

ICE
Cubes to shake, none to serve

GARNISH
Lime wedge

SERVES 1

40ml (1¼fl oz) Beefeater gin
25ml (¾fl oz) lime juice
15ml (½fl oz) Cointreau
5ml (1 tsp) sugar syrup
1 dash of orange bitters
1 dash of Angostura bitters

Bartender's Tip
You can infuse the sugar syrup with dried orange peel for a few days and omit the orange bitters from the recipe – this gives you a lighter, sweeter cocktail.

Add all the ingredients to a shaker with ice. Shake well, then strain into a chilled coupe glass and garnish with a lime wedge.

Ramos Gin Fizz

Henry C Ramos occupies something of a legendary status among bartenders. Tasteful to a fault, Ramos closed his bar, the Imperial Cabinet Saloon in New Orleans, at 8pm every night to prevent family men staying away from their wives and children, and would refuse to allow customers to become drunk on his cocktails. When Prohibition came into effect, Ramos forever closed the doors of his saloon at midnight on the dot, declaring that he'd sold his last gin fizz. The Ramos Gin Fizz is his legacy: a rich, delicious, refreshing drink that is notoriously arduous to make – it takes 12 minutes of shaking before serving.

GLASSWARE
Highball

ICE
Cubes to shake, none to serve

GARNISH
Lime slice

SERVES 1

50ml (1¾fl oz) Jensen's
 Old Tom gin
15ml (½fl oz) lemon juice
15ml (½fl oz) lime juice
15ml (½fl oz) single cream
15ml (½fl oz) sugar syrup
4 drops of orange flower water
1 egg white
Soda water, to top up

Add all the ingredients to a shaker with ice, adding the egg white as the last ingredient. Shake vigorously for as long as you can. Strain into a chilled highball glass and gently add a little bit of soda water. Garnish with a lime slice.

Bartender's Tip
Depending on personal preference, shake with less ice for a richer, thicker texture.

The Gower

The Gower is a tribute to head chef Steve Gower at Bam-Bou restaurant in London – home of The Red Bar. His lifelong passion for chilli inspired me to create this hot aperitif. It can be tailor-made to the intensity you require – I recommend using medium-strength chilli to begin with – and is a perfect companion to Asian-themed salads or appetizers. The slightly salty garlic works similarly to an olive, and can be a delicious treat at the end of the drink.

GLASSWARE
Martini

ICE
Cubes to stir, none to serve

GARNISH
Pickled garlic clove

SERVES 1

60ml (2fl oz) infused Tanqueray Dry gin (*see* below)
10ml (2 tsp) Martini Extra Dry

For the infused Tanqueray gin (Makes 1 bottle)
1 rosemary sprig
½ medium-strength chilli, cut lengthways
1 long strip of lemon peel
1 stalk of lemon grass, roughly chopped
1 bottle Tanqueray Dry gin

Bartender's Tip
Many Martini-style drinks are ruined by being served too warm, or worse, with a last-minute addition of ice! Drink by holding the stem of your Martini glass to keep it cold for as long as possible.

To infuse the gin, put the rosemary sprig, chilli, lemon peel and chopped lemon grass into the bottle of gin and leave to infuse for 24 hours. You do not need to strain the contents before using. Once you have used about half the bottle, you can top up with fresh gin. The rosemary, chilli, lemon peel and lemon grass will keep their flavour for about 3 more of these refills.

To make the cocktail, add the gin infusion and Martini Extra Dry to a mixing glass with ice. Stir well, then strain into a chilled Martini glass containing a pickled garlic clove.

Late Night Club

This is a twist on the classic Clover Club Cocktail and is especially delicious when raspberries are in full season. Bombay Original is a much drier version of its more famous stablemate Bombay Sapphire, and has stronger tones of juniper, which helps it stand out better against the fresh fruits in this recipe. Rose tea syrup and rosewater will help to bring the floral notes out, which make the cocktail complex and unique.

GLASSWARE
Coupe

ICE
Cubes to shake, none to serve

GARNISH
Dried pineapple or rose petal

SERVES 1

40ml (1¼fl oz) Bombay
  Original gin
20ml (¾fl oz) pineapple juice
20ml (¾fl oz) lime juice
15ml (½fl oz) rose tea syrup
  (*see* below)
3 fresh raspberries
1 dash of rosewater

For the rose tea syrup
Dried edible rose petals
100ml (3½fl oz) boiling water
200g (7oz) caster sugar

Bartender's Tip
Play around with the balance of flavours in this drink by experimenting with infusing the rose tea syrup or gin with raspberries.

First make the rose tea syrup. Steep the rose petals in the boiling water for several minutes. Add the sugar and stir until it has dissolved, then leave to infuse and cool. Strain, then bottle in a sterilized container until ready to use.

To make the cocktail, add all the ingredients to a shaker with ice. Shake well, then strain through a tea strainer into a chilled coupe glass. Garnish with a piece of dried pineapple or a rose petal.

Oscar

Originally created for a global cocktail competition, this fresh concoction makes you want to have another one as soon as the first is finished. Tanqueray No. TEN is a premium gin from one of the oldest gin distilleries in England, made with fresh citrus fruits such as grapefruit and lime. This helps to pair it with the more 'zingy' flavours of mandarin, tart kumquats and sweet notes of pomegranate.

GLASSWARE
Rocks

ICE
Cubes to shake and to serve

GARNISH
Dried lime slice, kumquat slice, mandarin twist

SERVES 1

1 kumquat, halved
45ml (1½fl oz) Tanqueray No. TEN gin
20ml (¾fl oz) lime juice
10ml (2 tsp) Mandarine Napoleon
10ml (2 tsp) pomegranate syrup

Muddle half the kumquat in the bottom of a shaker, then add the remaining ingredients and ice cubes. Shake well, then strain into a chilled rocks glass. Slice the remaining kumquat half and use to garnish, along with a lime slice and a mandarin twist.

Bartender's Tip
The Oscar can also be delicious when served without ice and just a splash of chilled champagne. For presentation points, serve this augmented version in a flute glass.

Prudence Of Hammersmith

Technically a Collins–style drink, this is very refreshing on a hot summer's day. Bergamot orange is a citrus fruit that is similar to a grapefruit and a lemon combined, and it is one of the key flavours in Earl Grey tea. Sipsmith gin was launched in Hammersmith in 2009 and proudly holds the first distilling licence granted in central London for nearly 200 years. This cocktail is named for the Sipsmith copper still, Prudence.

GLASSWARE
Highball

ICE
Cubes to serve

GARNISH
Lemon twist, lavender petals

SERVES 1

30ml (1fl oz) Sipsmith gin
20ml (¾fl oz) apricot liqueur
80ml (2½fl oz) chilled Earl Grey tea
15ml (½fl oz) Bergamot sherbet (*see* below)
15ml (½fl oz) lemon juice

For the Bergamot sherbet (Makes 200ml/7fl oz)
zest and juice of **2** Bergamot oranges
150g (5oz) caster sugar

You will also need
Soda siphon and carbon dioxide charges

Bartender's Tip
Bergamot is a fantastic citrus fruit, but it is only available for a limited season. Out of season, you can substitute with pink grapefruit, which I have found works beautifully.

First make the sherbet. Muddle together the Bergamot zest and caster sugar in a bowl to release the oils from the grated zest. Add the Bergamot juice and stir until the sugar has dissolved, then strain through a tea strainer. Keep refrigerated until ready to use.

Measure all the ingredients into a soda siphon and charge with carbon dioxide. Pour the mixture into a highball glass over ice. Garnish with dried lemon and lavender petals.

Three Plus Three Martini

This aperitif is a fantastic way to kick off dinner. No.3 is a gin created by Berry Bros. & Rudd, London's oldest wine merchants. Made with only three spices and three fruits, it has remarkable balance. By adding savoury notes from green plum and artichoke liqueurs, this recipe highlights the citrus character of the gin, creating a Martini that is very appetizing and moreish.

GLASSWARE
Martini

ICE
Cubes to stir, none to serve

GARNISH
Grapefruit twist

SERVES 1

50ml (1¾fl oz) No.3 gin
15ml (½fl oz) Akashi-Tai Shiruame Umeshu (plum sake liqueur)
5ml (1 tsp) Cynar
2 dashes of Bitter Truth grapefruit bitters

Add all the ingredients to a mixing glass with ice. Stir well, then strain into a chilled Martini glass. Garnish with a grapefruit twist.

Bartender's Tip
Don't go too heavy on the Cynar – use only precisely the amount I recommend. This artichoke liqueur has an extremely strong flavour and can unbalance the whole cocktail if there's too much of it.

Yeoman Warder

This is a twist on the famous Negroni, utilizing Aperol and ratafia, which are sweet, bitter liqueurs. Beefeater 24 is a premium citrus- and Japanese Sencha tea-based London Dry gin and is less juniper-driven than the original Beefeater gin. Yeoman Warders is the official name of the Beefeaters, the ceremonial guards at the Tower of London.

GLASSWARE
Rocks

ICE
Cubes to stir, large cube to serve

GARNISH
Dried orange slice

SERVES 1

30ml (1fl oz) Beefeater 24 gin
20ml (¾fl oz) Aperol
10ml (2 tsp) Evangelista ratafia
1 dash of Bob's orange & mandarin bitters

Bartender's Tip
All the ingredients for the Yeoman Warder can be pre-measured and bottled together. Just refrigerate and you have a great aperitif ready to serve on ice when your guests appear unexpectedly.

Add all the ingredients to a mixing glass with ice. Stir well, then strain into a rocks glass containing a large ice cube. Garnish with a dried orange slice.

Gin Tea Punch

Punch as a mixed drink became popular in England after being brought back from India in the early 17th century. Sailors would be given their rum rations mixed with citrus juice in order to ward off scurvy, and officers often enjoyed this mixture as a formal drink. While the English were travelling and exploring the New World, they were also gaining access to new spices, citrus fruits and other ingredients. My Gin Tea Punch is inspired by two of the nation's favourite drinks: gin and tea. Bergamot is the key flavour in Earl Grey tea and works very well with Hendrick's gin, which is known for its cucumber and rose petal flavours.

GLASSWARE
Teacup

ICE
Cubes to shake, large cube to serve

GARNISH
Cucumber slices, mint leaves, lemon slice, raspberry

SERVES 1

35ml (1fl oz) Hendrick's gin
15ml (½fl oz) Cointreau
40ml (1¼fl oz) Earl Grey tea
1 tbsp Bergamot Sherbet
    (*see* page 23)
1 tsp apricot jam

Add all the ingredients to a shaker with ice. Shake well, until the apricot jam has broken up and dissolved. Strain into a teacup containing a single large ice cube. Garnish with the cucumber, mint, lemon slice and a fresh raspberry.

Bartender's Tip
This drink multiplies well: when served in a big, classic punchbowl, it's perfect for a party or a picnic. It can also easily be topped up with sparkling wine to make it a little more exciting.

An Affair To Remember

I created this drink on the spur of the moment for a couple sitting at the bar, enjoying a few cocktails together while celebrating their wedding anniversary. The challenge of naming the drink was the most difficult part! The young lady said, 'I know, let's name it after that movie with Deborah Kerr and Cary Grant, but I can't remember its name.' Another couple, overhearing our plight and intrigued by our conundrum, interjected: '*An Affair to Remember*' – a romantic name for a romantic drink.

GLASSWARE
Sherry or Martini

ICE
Cubes to shake, none to serve

GARNISH
Peychaud's bitters, dried rosebuds

SERVES 1

35ml (1fl oz) Bombay Sapphire gin
15ml (½fl oz) dry cherry liqueur
20ml (¾fl oz) lemon juice
20ml (¾fl oz) pink grapefruit juice
1 tbsp caster sugar
1 egg white

Add all the ingredients to a shaker with ice, adding the egg white as the last ingredient. Shake vigorously, then strain into a sherry or Martini glass, add drops of Peychaud's bitters to the surface to taste and garnish with a few rosebuds.

Bartender's Tip
For a bit of fun, let your guests try to guess the name of this drink (from the description above) before you tell them what it is. It works... trust me!

'I believe that if life gives you lemons, you should make lemonade... And try to find somebody whose life has given them vodka, and have a party.'
American comedian
Ron White

Recipes by Gareth Evans

Social Eating House, London

Vodka
by John Naughton

Some claim vodka as Poland's, while others swear its provenance is entirely Russian. What is not in doubt is that for centuries, if you needed to get the party started in the *shtetl* or the Winter Palace, from Poznań to St Petersburg, vodka was the weapon of choice.

There is evidence of the spirit's existence as early as the 9th century, but the argument about its origins is far from academic. In 1979 – some years before glasnost – the Polish government attempted to sue the mighty Soviet Union to prove that the drink was first distilled on Polish soil and to gain exclusive commercial rights to the word 'vodka'. Perhaps predictably, the Poles lost the case, which enabled Stolichnaya to claim in its advertising, 'Only vodka from Russia is genuine Russian vodka.' Not such a great boast when you come to think about it.

These days, both countries successfully produce a range of vodkas, which is hardly surprising because the market is enormous. Global consumption of vodka in 2012 was almost 4.5 billion litres (1 billion imperial gallons), with Russia alone accounting for 2 billion litres (440 million imperial gallons) of that, which works out at 14 litres (3 imperial gallons) for every man, woman and highly intoxicated child. Not only does Russia drink the most, but it also boasts the biggest brands, with Smirnoff the market leader and, by some calculations, the best-selling premium spirit in the world.

The drink's worldwide success is not simply down to thirsty Russians, however. Adding a range of flavours to this traditionally neutral drink has proved a canny marketing tool, and the likes of Stolichnaya and Smirnoff have struck gold (literally) with every flavour from chocolate raspberry to cinnamon with gold leaf. Yet it is instructive to study what is undoubtedly at the root of vodka's modern appeal – its versatility in cocktails.

While the history of vodka in cocktails goes back much further (some say Bloody Marys were being mixed as early as 1921), it makes sense to trace the spirit's first modern spike in popularity to a particularly successful spy and his distinctive drink. James Bond's badge of individuality was his vodka Martini. As well as famously preferring it 'shaken and not stirred', which was unconventional, 007 showed his real iconoclasm by demanding vodka in a drink traditionally seen as a simple mixture of gin and vermouth. Bond's original cocktail, which he christened a Vesper Martini after femme fatale Vesper Lynd and first ordered in chapter seven of *Casino Royale*, comprised 'three measures of Gordon's, one of vodka, half a measure of Kina Lillet [a brand of vermouth]. Shake it very well until it's ice-cold, then add a large, thin slice of lemon peel.'

For reasons that no one seems able to explain, vodka has always benefited from a degree of celebrity endorsement. Take the Cosmopolitan, introduced originally as a ladies' version of the straight Martini by bartender Cheryl Cook at The Strand restaurant in South Beach, Florida, in 1985. A mix of Absolut Citron, triple sec, Rose's Lime Juice and cranberry juice, it developed a loyal

Q&A with
Gareth Evans

How long have you been a bartender? Long enough that my Mum has accepted that I'm not going to be a lawyer – 13 years.

What is your bartending philosophy? Drinks have to make sense; the name, presentation and ingredients must work together and tell a story, and not just be random things from the backbar with a fancy garnish. I know that sounds very pretentious, but a story is the reason drinks get remembered.

What is your favourite cocktail ingredient at the moment (and why)? Apricot brandy. Impossible to make a bad drink with it. It's bartender gaffer tape; it fixes everything.

Where can drinkers try your creations? Social Eating House, Pollen Street Social, Little Social and Berners Tavern, all in London, as well as Jason Atherton's many outposts in Asia.

Three great all-rounder vodkas recommended by Gareth Evans

1 Ketel One (Dutch)
2 Stolichnaya (Russian)
3 Black Cow (English)

following. But it only really took off when Dale DeGroff, aka 'King Cocktail', tweaked it, introduced it to the Rainbow Room in New York and then made sure Madonna was spotted drinking one in 1996 at a Grammy awards party. Nor was its profile hurt when it became the drink of choice for the chief protagonists in the TV programme *Sex and the City*.

On the other side of the Atlantic, Stolichnaya, or Stoli as it rapidly became known, was the natural rhyming accompaniment to Bollinger (Bolly) on the 1990s sitcom *Absolutely Fabulous*, even spawning the inevitable cocktail combination (a Stoli Bolly), upon which no one as yet has appeared willing to bestow classic status. Nevertheless, given the show's international success, it proved a huge boost to the Russian brand's profile worldwide. Ironically, given the show's popularity within the gay community, this high profile made Stoli the object of an attempted worldwide boycott in 2013 in order to highlight Russian discrimination against the country's LGBT community.

Of course, there is a school of thought that to drink vodka in cocktails is to miss the point entirely. Vodka purists insist that the best (indeed only) way to drink it is frozen and neat. Those wishing to try out this theory should keep the vodka bottle in the freezer, then place the glasses alongside it for an hour. When the glass is sufficiently chilled, pour out a measure (never over ice) and hold the glass in your hand, allowing it to warm up just a little to release the more intense flavours. Connoisseurs should also consider the look of the drink, with better-quality vodkas exhibiting a creamy, viscous quality, and even emitting a bluish glow when held up to the light (although this might be open to debate). Keep the palate entertained between sips with salty snacks and fish – a bracing rollmop herring is particularly recommended.

Whether frozen or in cocktails, it makes sense to drink only better-quality vodkas. What's lost in the wallet is gained in the intensity of the hangover. No one should ignore a couple of Polish classics; Chopin, a potato-based vodka, as smooth as one would expect of a product named after the composer of the Nocturnes; a special mention too for Belvedere – the sight of one of its distinctively frosted bottles behind a bar is guaranteed to gladden the heart of true vodkaphiles. Stoli (whose Blueberi flavour demands to be tried) and Zyr will fight the Russian corner admirably in this market (probably best to give Kalashnikov a miss). But if you want evidence that the field is no longer dominated by these two old adversaries, then go Dutch. Try Van Gogh Blue or the beautifully smooth Ketel One and leave your Russian and Polish friends to argue it out among themselves.

Bloody Mary

The origins of the most famous of savoury cocktails are by no means clear; however, most cocktail experts tend to lean towards one story – that of Fernand 'Pete' Petiot, who was said to have developed the drink in the early Twenties while working at Harry's New York Bar in Paris. After Prohibition, Petiot moved to Manhattan and the King Cole Bar at the St. Regis hotel, where the Bloody Mary was temporarily renamed the Red Snapper.

GLASSWARE
Highball

ICE
Cubes to throw and to serve

GARNISH
Celery stick, 2 cherry tomatoes, lemon slice, cracked black pepper

SERVES 1

50ml (1¾fl oz) Chase vodka
125ml (4fl oz) tomato juice
15ml (½fl oz) Worcestershire sauce
15ml (½fl oz) lemon juice
4 dashes of Tabasco sauce
1 pinch of celery salt
1 pinch of freshly grated black pepper
2.5cm (1in) piece of fresh horseradish, grated

Take two cocktail shakers and in one add all the ingredients and ice cubes. Using a strainer carefully pour the mixture back and forth between the shakers 4–5 times, then strain into a chilled highball glass over ice. Garnish with a stick of celery, 2 cherry tomatoes, a lemon slice and some cracked black pepper.

Bartender's Tip
Variations on this drink are endless, but I like to swap out the vodka for mescal, and add a dash of Tabasco chipotle sauce for a smoky version of a Bloody Maria (*see* page 83).

Cosmopolitan

Another cocktail with a disputed history, the Cosmopolitan is said to have been created by Cheryl Cook (*see* page 32). The drink as we know it today has two reluctant parents, Toby Cecchini (who developed the drink with cranberry juice, lemon vodka and Cointreau) and Dale DeGroff (who is said to have introduced fresh lime juice and the drink's signature flamed orange peel garnish). The reputation of the 'Cosmo' has taken a bit of a battering in recent years due to bad replications and TV overexposure, but made properly this is a great drink: sharp, tart and boozy.

GLASSWARE
Martini or wine

ICE
Cubes to shake, none to serve

GARNISH
Flamed orange peel (discarded)

SERVES 1

40ml (1¼fl oz) Ketel One
   Citroen vodka
20ml (¾fl oz) triple sec
20ml (¾fl oz) lime juice
20ml (¾fl oz) cranberry juice

Add all the ingredients to a shaker with ice. Shake hard, then strain into a chilled Martini or wine glass. Slice a 2.5cm (1in) circle of orange peel. Holding a lit match above the surface of the drink, squeeze the peel quickly over the flame to release the oils into the drink (it will flame briefly), then discard the peel.

Bartender's Tip
The late-Nineties saw many different versions of this drink, most notably Ben Reed's Metropolitan using blackcurrant vodka.

Vodka Espresso

There's no doubting the lineage of this drink. Legendary UK bartender Dick Bradsell's signature has gone through several iterations and names over his career, but this is the most recognizable of its reincarnations. The story of the Vodka Espresso's creation is etched in the mind of all young bartenders; in Dick's own words: 'It was at the Soho Brasserie in the Eighties. A young American model asked for a drink that "wakes me up and then f**ks me up".' A great blend of flavour and creativity – the sort of simple, classic cocktail that just makes you ask: 'Why didn't I think of that?'

GLASSWARE
Coupe

ICE
Cubes to shake, none to serve

GARNISH
3 coffee beans

SERVES 1

50ml (1¾fl oz) Ketel One vodka
10ml (2 tsp) Kahlúa
5ml (1 tsp) sugar syrup
1 shot of fresh espresso

Add all the ingredients to a shaker with ice. Shake hard, then strain into a chilled coupe glass and garnish with the coffee beans.

Bartender's Tip
If you want to tweak proceedings a little, swap the sugar syrup for either Baileys Irish Cream liqueur or some white crème de cacao.

White Russian

One of the best of the creamy stable of drinks, this version was developed first from a drink called simply The Russian, which consists of vodka, gin and crème de cacao. The Russian appears in *The Savoy Cocktail Book* and speaks of a time when vodka was primarily imported from Russia. This then spawned the Black Russian, which is simply vodka and Kahlúa over ice. The addition of cream makes this drink very approachable, and its inclusion as the cocktail of choice for 'the Dude' (played by Jeff Bridges) in the 1998 cult film *The Big Lebowski* gave the White Russian retro credentials and a new lease of life.

GLASSWARE
Rocks

ICE
Large rock or cubes

GARNISH
None

SERVES 1

40ml (1¼fl oz) Black Cow vodka
20ml (¾fl oz) Kahlúa
20ml (¾fl oz) double cream

Build the vodka, Kahlúa and cream in a chilled rocks glass over ice and stir to combine.

Bartender's Tip
A popular variation is to add vanilla vodka and chocolate liqueur to make a Russian Bride, but my favourite is a bit kitsch – make the drink as usual, but add a top of cola to make a Colorado Bulldog. Don't knock it 'til you've tried it.

Vanilla Laika

Now qualifying as a modern vodka classic, this drink was created by UK bartending stalwart Jake Burger at Townhouse in Leeds back in 2002. The drink takes its name from Laika, the first dog in space, doomed by the Russian space programme to die in orbit aboard Sputnik 2. So raise a glass to the first canine to boldly go where no dog had gone before.

GLASSWARE
Collins or highball

ICE
Cubes to shake and to serve

GARNISH
Lemon wedge, blackberry, mint sprig

SERVES 1

40ml (1¼fl oz) Stolichnaya Vanil vodka
20ml (¾fl oz) crème de mûre
10ml (2 tsp) lemon juice
100ml (3½fl oz) cloudy apple juice

Add all the ingredients to a shaker with ice. Shake well, then strain into a chilled Collins or highball glass over ice. Garnish with a lemon wedge, a blackberry and a sprig of mint.

Bartender's Tip
This is a great formula, and can stand a lot of meddling and still taste great. Try adding a few fresh blackberries and a dash of Poire William for a thicker texture and a bit more of a winter flavour.

Caipiroska

On paper this is simply a version of the Brazilian national drink the Caipirinha (*see* Bartender's Tip), but the Caipiroska has become an essential part of any bartender's repertoire in recent years. Of course, we have been helped by the resurgence of craft vodkas that have made simple, tasty drinks such as this popular again. Add in the fact that anyone with a bag of ice, a lime and some table sugar can make a passable version without so much as a shaker and you have all the makings of a classic.

GLASSWARE
Rocks

ICE
Cubes and cracked ice to shake and to serve

GARNISH
Lime wedge

SERVES 1

6 lime wedges
15ml (½fl oz) sugar syrup
50ml (1¾fl oz) Ketel One vodka

Muddle the lime wedges with the syrup in the bottom of a shaker, then add the vodka and cubed and cracked ice. Shake hard, then pour all the contents into a chilled rocks glass. Garnish with a lime wedge.

Bartender's Tip
This drink works with almost any spirit swapped with the vodka: cachaça (a sugar-cane spirit) for an original Caipirinha, or rum for a Caipirissima, but I like to use Campari to make a great bittersweet aperitif – the Camparinha.

Moscow Mule

The Moscow Mule came about due to slick marketing and over-ordering. The story goes that in 1941 John G Martin of Heublein Inc., a spirits company which had acquired the rights to Smirnoff vodka in the USA, conspired with Jack Morgan, owner of the Cock 'n' Bull Tavern in Los Angeles, who had a surplus of ginger beer. Together, they created a cocktail using their ingredients and a dash of fresh lime and marketed the drink to bartenders using copper mugs. An instant classic was born: approachable, recognizable and simple enough to be recreated in pretty much any bar.

GLASSWARE
Copper mug or highball

ICE
Cubes

GARNISH
Lime wedge, edible flowers

SERVES 1

50ml (1¾fl oz) Ketel One vodka
dash of Angostura bitters
15ml (½fl oz) lime juice
Ginger beer, to top up

Build the vodka, bitters and lime juice in a chilled copper mug or highball glass over ice, adding the ginger beer last. Stir to combine and garnish with a lime wedge and edible flowers.

Bartender's Tip
This drink is great for playing about with – try throwing the vodka, lime and bitters in a shaker with a few raspberries and a bit of mint, then shake and top up with the ginger beer over ice in a highball glass.

Mile High Club

Loosely based on a Clover Club cocktail, I came up with this light, tart cocktail for a competition that took place on board a flight to New York – hence the name. The 'dry shake' before adding ice whips up the egg white and gives the drink its aerated texture, and the bitter notes of the rhubarb and Aperol contrast with the sour lemon and sweetness of the elderflower liqueur.

GLASSWARE
Martini or coupe

ICE
Cubes to shake, none to serve

GARNISH
Bitters

SERVES 1

40ml (1¼fl oz) Ketel One vodka
15ml (½fl oz) Aperol
15ml (½fl oz) Chase elderflower
liqueur
10ml (2 tsp) rhubarb syrup
25ml (¾fl oz) lemon juice
½ egg white

Add all the ingredients to a shaker (without ice) and dry shake briefly, but vigorously, to fluff up the egg white (*see* page 219). Add ice and shake again. Strain into a chilled Martini or coupe glass and garnish by spraying bitters over the drink's surface.

Bartender's Tip
To add a nice visual element and change the aroma of this drink, serve with a 'vanilla amaro' spray: equal parts Fernet Branca, Angostura bitters and vanilla bitters, sprayed in an oil mister through a stencil on the surface of the drink.

Breakfast Fizz

With this drink the intention was to create a cocktail with all the flavours associated with the ideal breakfast: grapefruit, honey, marmalade and, of course, sparkling wine! I love to use British ingredients where I can, and Nyetimber is a great example of an English producer creating excellent sparkling wines. The south of England has perfect conditions for growing the high-acidity Chardonnay grapes used to produce the Blanc de Blancs.

GLASSWARE
Wine

ICE
Cubes to shake, none to serve

GARNISH
Slice of toast, grapefruit marmalade

SERVES 1

40ml (1¼fl oz) Chase marmalade vodka
20ml (¾fl oz) yellow Chartreuse
40ml (1¼fl oz) pink grapefruit juice
Nyetimber Blanc de Blancs, to top up

Bartender's Tip
The Nyetimber here works well with the ingredients, but feel free to substitute it if you prefer. Asti would suit those with sweeter palates, or you could use soda water for something a little less boozy.

Add all the ingredients except the champagne to a shaker with ice. Shake, then strain into a chilled wine glass, top up with Nyetimber fizz and stir briefly. Garnish with a small slice of toast spread with grapefruit marmalade.

The Professor

This cocktail was invented for one of our most loyal regulars, who is both a professor of sociology and a fan of bitter, aperitif-style drinks such as Negronis. Every time she came in for a year or so we would make a slightly different version of this drink until one day she decided we had nailed the recipe, so it went on the menu – and has stayed there ever since. I used Chase Smoked vodka for a rounded mouthfeel and a nice flavour from the oak smoke, along with Barolo Chinato (a fortified wine with added bitter notes from quinine) and Kamm & Sons, a great ginseng-based bitter spirit created by a UK bartender.

GLASSWARE
Coupe

ICE
Cubes to stir, none to serve

GARNISH
Grapefruit twist

SERVES 1

25ml (¾fl oz) Chase smoked vodka
25ml (¾fl oz) Barolo Chinato
25ml (¾fl oz) Kamm & Sons
3 dashes of Dr Adam Elmegirab's dandelion & burdock bitters

Add all the ingredients to a mixing glass with ice. Stir well, then strain into a chilled coupe glass. Garnish with a grapefruit twist.

Bartender's Tip
Try changing the vodka to a bright gin such as Portobello Road for a more approachable tipple, or change the Barolo Chinato for a softer type of fortified wine such as Carpano Antica Formula, or even Cocchi Rosa.

Eurozone Negroni

Created for the opening of chef Jason Atherton's French bistro Little Social in London, this light, Negroni-style aperitif cocktail uses citrus vodka in place of gin, teamed with Suze (a bitter French liqueur slightly reminiscent of Campari) and white vermouth. The French theme was completed with a dash of absinthe. Absinthe is a polarizing ingredient, but I am a big fan of using it in very small amounts as you would bitters, where it acts almost like a seasoning for the drink.

GLASSWARE
Rocks

ICE
Cubes to stir and to serve

GARNISH
Lemon twist

SERVES 1

25ml (¾fl oz) Ketel One Citroen vodka
25ml (¾fl oz) Suze
25ml (¾fl oz) Gancia Bianco vermouth
5ml (1 tsp) absinthe, plus a dash to wash the glass

Add all the ingredients to a mixing glass with ice and stir. Add a dash of absinthe to a chilled rocks glass, swirl round and discard. Strain the cocktail into the absinthe-washed glass over ice. Garnish with a lemon twist.

Bartender's Tip
Feel free to omit the absinthe if you are not a fan of anise, or try adding a dash of bitter lemon or soda and a slice of grapefruit to make a longer, more refreshing, cooler style of drink.

Honey, I'm Home

Another drink using Ketel One Citroen, this time twisting the Bee's Knees cocktail, originally made with gin. The lemon notes of the vodka work very well with the full-flavoured manuka honey. Manuka trees are native to Australia and New Zealand, and the honey produced is the most viscous of all cultivated honeys, giving a great mouthfeel to the finished drink. Honey in general – and especially the super-thick manuka – doesn't dissolve well in cold alcohol, so it's important to dissolve the honey in the lemon prior to shaking.

GLASSWARE
Coupe

ICE
Cubes to shake, none to serve

GARNISH
Honeycomb

SERVES 1

10ml (2 tsp) manuka honey
25ml (¾fl oz) lemon juice
50ml (1¾fl oz) Ketel One Citroen vodka
1 dash of orange bitters

Add the honey and lemon juice to the bottom of a shaker and stir to dissolve. Add the vodka, bitters and ice and shake hard. Strain into a chilled coupe glass and garnish with a piece of honeycomb.

Bartender's Tip
Any sort of honey can be used for this cocktail, although it's not to be underestimated how much effect this will have on the final result.

The Rosefield

This drink was born when we tried to make a stirred down, Manhattan-style drink using lighter, less traditional ingredients. The English spiced vermouth is a great counterbalance to the lighter orange flavour of the vodka, and I am a sucker for any drink with either apricot brandy or Fernet Branca in it. The apricot adds a lovely deep fruity flavour and the bitter menthol hit from the powerful Fernet acts like a dash of bitters in a Manhattan, serving to lift the other flavours and adding a slightly savoury edge to cut the sweetness of the other ingredients.

GLASSWARE
Rocks

ICE
Cubes to stir, large sphere or rock to serve

GARNISH
Grapefruit wedge, fresh cherry

SERVES 1

50ml (1¾fl oz) Chase marmalade vodka
20ml (¾fl oz) Sacred Spiced English vermouth
10ml (2 tsp) apricot brandy
5ml (1 tsp) Fernet Branca

Add all the ingredients to a mixing glass with ice. Stir, then strain into a chilled rocks glass containing a large ice sphere. Garnish with a grapefruit wedge and a cherry.

Bartender's Tip
Try swapping the vermouth for something lighter or drier, such as Lillet Blanc, and try changing the apricot brandy to maraschino liqueur for a completely different type of drink.

My Word!

This vodka drink is a twist on the Prohibition-era cocktail the Last Word developed at the Detroit Athletic Club (first mentioned in Ted Saucier's bar book *Bottoms Up* in 1951). The herbal yellow Chartreuse is sweeter and less punchy than the traditional green counterpart, and the dry maraschino liqueur adds another layer to the cocktail.

GLASSWARE
Sherry or wine

ICE
Cubes to shake, none to serve

GARNISH
None

SERVES 1

20ml (¾fl oz) Ketel One Citroen vodka
20ml (¾fl oz) yellow Chartreuse
20ml (¾fl oz) maraschino liqueur
20ml (¾fl oz) lime juice

Bartender's Tip
To try the original Last Word, swap the vodka for a London Dry gin, and go for the traditional Chartreuse (green) instead of the yellow.

Add all the ingredients to a shaker with ice. Shake, then strain into a chilled sherry or wine glass.

Vintage Vesper

This cocktail stems from the classic Vesper cocktail requested by James Bond in Ian Fleming's spy novel *Casino Royale*, consisting of vodka, gin and Kina Lillet (a now defunct bitter aperitif wine). My version uses aged spirits to add complexity and depth, as well as Cocchi Americano, an aperitif wine said to be the closest modern variation of the Kina Lillet that Bond was so fond of. This cocktail is unusual as most drinks not containing citrus juice tend to be stirred to provide a smooth mouthfeel. However, this one is shaken to add a more lively texture and to ensure that the drink is super cold. 007 would surely approve.

GLASSWARE
Coupe or Martini

ICE
Cubes to shake, none to serve

GARNISH
Lemon peel (discarded)

SERVES 1

40ml (1¼fl oz) Adnams North Cove oak-aged vodka
25ml (¾fl oz) Citadelle Reserve gin
20ml (¾fl oz) Cocchi Americano

Add all the ingredients to a shaker with ice. Shake, then strain into a chilled coupe or Martini glass. Zest the lemon peel to release the oils over the surface of the drink (*see* page 219), then wipe the peel around the rim and either discard or use to garnish.

Bartender's Tip
One of the reasons mixologists claim that a Martini shouldn't be shaken is that this can leave small shards of ice on the surface. To avoid this here, use a very fine strainer when you pour the drink.

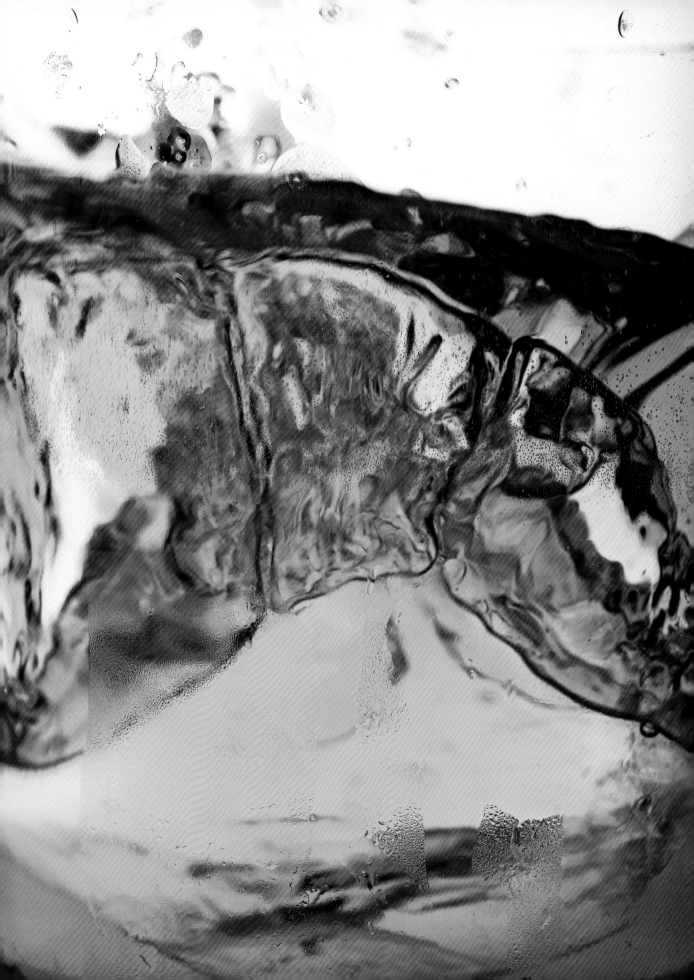

'I pity them greatly,
but I must be mum,
for how could we do
without sugar and rum?'
William Cowper

Recipes by Milos Popovic

Old Bengal Bar, London

Rum
by Jennifer Bradly

Rum. Whether it is light, gold, dark, black, spiced, overproof or straight-from-the-still moonshine from a Jamaican shack bar, it has come a long way to get into your glass.

It started 8,000 years ago as sugar cane – *Saccharum officinarum*, a grass native to New Guinea – which slowly made its way across the globe via Southeast Asia, India, Africa and Spain, and was eventually traded as an expensive spice and medicine. It was Columbus who first introduced sugar cane to the New World – the island of Hispaniola – in 1493, on his second voyage, having picked up the cuttings in the Canary Islands. By the early 16th century the crop had been taken by the Spanish and Portuguese to the other Caribbean islands and to Central and South America.

Having arrived in the Caribbean, sugar would flavour the islands' history. The cultivation of the canes required a huge workforce, so in the early 16th century the first African slaves were forced to labour in Hispaniola's sugar-cane fields, a practice that would rip through the Caribbean over the next three centuries. Sugar and slavery became shackled together.

And rum? A version of the spirit was recorded in the 1620s in Brazil, and a substance thought to be rum was found aboard the Swedish warship *Vasa*, which sank in 1628. But it was the sugar plantations of the Caribbean that kick-started the rise of rum as we know it. By the mid-17th century, those who had acquired a taste for the good life turned their thoughts to molasses, the gloopy liquid by-product of sugar manufacturing. Could this be a moneymaker too? What was not fed to slaves and livestock was just being dumped into the sea, until a bright spark realized that it could be distilled into liquid gold – well, cane spirit. This became rudimentary rum, and before long every plantation across the Caribbean had its own copper pot still.

Rum's etymology is as murky as a distiller's dunder pit. It wasn't even called rum at first. *Eau de vie*, some named it, or *aguardiente*. Etymologist Samuel Morewood suggested in 1824 that 'rum' stemmed from the slang for 'great', as in 'having a rum time', but others disagree – not least because early rum was so harsh ('a hot, hellish and terrible liquor,' gasped one anonymous victim). Was it from the last syllable of *saccharum*? Freebooted from the Romani word for 'potent'? A truncated form of *rumbullion*, meaning a great tempest or an uproar, or perhaps derived from the Dutch seaman's drinking vessel, the *rummer*? The etymological explanations are as numerous as the brands of rum available today.

Back in the 1600s, while planters sipped brandy, slaves drank the rough, early rum as a pick-me-up. But as distillation methods were refined, the flavour improved and the spirit became fashionable back in England. The British Royal Navy even rationed rum to its sailors from 1655 to 1970, though from 1740 it was often diluted, to become 'grog'. Planters' pockets overflowed, thanks to mass production: human flesh exchanged for rum.

Q&A with Milos Popovic

Describe your current bar?
A beautiful hidden gem with great food, amazing drinks and fabulous staff/service. Oh, and it has a great cigar terrace, too.

Who was your mentor/bartending inspiration? A wise man once said, 'If you are going to do something in your life, do it properly or don't do it at all.' I think that sums it up.

What is your bartending philosophy? Simplicity and customer service are the key.

What is the key to making a great cocktail? Passion, skills and good ingredients.

Where can drinkers try your creations? Currently at the Old Bengal Bar in the City of London.

What would be the cocktail you would drink on your deathbed? I hope for some nice rum punch with a big cocktail umbrella served by a bartender who happens to work at the beach bar on one of Caribbean islands.

Three great all-rounder rums recommended by Milos Popovic

1 Diplomático Reserva Exclusiva (Venezuelan)
2 Ron Zacapa 23yo (Guatemalan)
3 Appleton Estate (Jamaican)

This taste for rum endured, and by the 1830s, Jamaica was making more money from the spirit than from sugar. Lighter, drier rum styles evolved to compete with the traditional darker types. Over the century that followed, rum rode out fluctuations in fashion, flourished in the hands of organized crime during the US Prohibition (the 1920–33 booze ban made people thirstier than ever) and survived – just – the Great Depression of the 1930s. At that time, drinkers could choose between Jamaican, Cuban, French or Demerara rum. But by the 1960s the brand was all: Captain Morgan, Lamb's, Black Heart. Bacardi had become an international frontrunner (and still is, though the Philippine company Tanduay is hot on its heels). Bacardi was ejected from Cuba by Fidel Castro, who seized their production facilities in 1960, and by the time the 1990s rolled around, the brand was engaged in a fraught 'rum war' with the US-embargoed Cuban brand Havana Club.

Rum, it seems, will never stray far from political drama, but still it booms. While it is mainly made in the Caribbean and Latin America, it is also produced in Spain, North America, East Asia, Australia and New Zealand. Sales now top $2 billion a year in the USA alone. What is more, a cobwebbed collection of a dozen bottles of rum dating back to 1780, discovered in Leeds, UK, sold for an unprecedented £78,255 at Christie's in December 2013. So how does that syrupy, waste-product goo become this delicious, auction-busting, world-changing spirit?

Gradual evolution and local traditions mean that rum, unlike most spirits, has no strictly defined production method. Yeast and water are added to molasses (or to crushed sugar-cane juice in the case of the rarer, French *rhum agricole*) to begin fermentation. The type of yeast goes some way to determining the rum's flavour and aroma: the faster-working it is, the lighter the rum. The liquid is then distilled – that is, heated to release alcohol vapours that are condensed into a spirit. This is usually done in column stills but, for a fuller-tasting product, traditional pot stills are sometimes used.

For most rums, the maturation process comes next: ageing the spirit, usually in oak bourbon barrels, which lend the liquid its tannins, its signature flavours of vanilla, coconut, tobacco, citrus peel or spice, and its colour. In a tropical climate, the liquor evaporates more quickly and matures up to three times faster than it does in cooler areas, so when it comes to rum, age certainly is more than a number. The more mature the rum, of course, the darker it is. And the number of times the cask has been used previously also influences the rum's flavour profile, giving producers even more opportunity for variety. The master blender then determines the rum's ultimate taste, blending not to a specific recipe – there are too many variables for that – but to the desired flavour, perhaps mixing light column-still rum with heavier pot-still rum or even water, revealing hidden aromas.

The finished product is one of the most diverse and versatile spirits in the world. Whether you sip it straight up or, as you will see in the pages that follow, lay it down as the sweet foundation for cocktails, rum's inimitable flavours and rich history mean that it can always be relied upon to bring its own character to the party.

Dark 'n' Stormy

Taking its name from a sailor who, on surveying the drink before him, described it as being 'the colour of a cloud only a fool or a dead man would sail under', the Dark 'n' Stormy is a classic cocktail that is part of the Mule family (see page 41). The key with this simple libation is to get the right balance between the strong and punchy rum and the sweet and spicy ginger beer. Nail that, and the forecast will look very good.

GLASSWARE
Highball

ICE
Cubes to shake and to serve

GARNISH
Lime slice

SERVES 1

50ml (1¾fl oz) Gosling's Black Seal rum
3–4 lime wedges
Ginger beer, to top up

Bartender's Tip
Dark 'n' Stormy is the national drink of Bermuda, but to do it their way you need to leave out the lime.

Add the rum and lime wedges to a shaker with ice. Shake, then strain into a chilled highball glass over ice and top up with ginger beer. Garnish with a lime slice.

Plantation Daiquiri

Like so many cocktails, the origins of the Daiquiri are hotly debated, but credit seems to be given to an American mining engineer called Jennings Cox. Depending on who you believe, Cox either invented the drink with the help of another engineer in 1896, or because he ran out of gin while entertaining in 1905. Either way, as a celebration of light rum it is hard to beat this cocktail when shaken hard with equal parts of fresh lime juice and sugar syrup. Serve it straight up.

GLASSWARE
Coupe

ICE
Cubes to shake, none to serve

GARNISH
None

SERVES 1

50ml (1¾fl oz) Plantation 3 Stars silver rum
25ml (¾fl oz) sugar syrup
25ml (¾fl oz) lime juice

Bartender's Tip
All Daiquiris listed are actually a variation on the original Daiquiri and its famous ratio of 50/25/25 of white rum/lime juice/ sugar syrup, but what is essential is that citrus juices are squeezed fresh.

Add all the ingredients to a shaker with ice. Shake vigorously, then strain into a chilled coupe glass.

The Painkiller

This cocktail was inspired by Daphne Henderson, owner of the six-seat Soggy Dollar Bar at White Bay on Jost Van Dyke. The bar gets its name because there is no dock for sailors to berth their boats, so they have no choice but to swim ashore (hence their wet cash). No real hardship in the British Virgin Islands, we'll admit, but you don't need to be in the Caribbean to enjoy this smooth tropical tipple, and this version is as close to Daphne's very secret recipe as possible (I hope).

GLASSWARE
Hurricane

ICE
Cubes to shake, crushed ice to serve

GARNISH
Grated nutmeg, orange slice, pineapple leaf

SERVES 1

50ml (1¾fl oz) Pusser's rum
25ml (¾fl oz) pineapple juice
25ml (¾fl oz) orange juice
15ml (½fl oz) Coco López coconut cream

Bartender's Tip
For a sweeter, smoother version, feel free to double up on the pineapple juice.

Add all the ingredients to a shaker with ice. Shake and strain into a chilled hurricane glass over crushed ice. Garnish with a grated nutmeg, an orange slice and a pineapple leaf.

El Presidente

Another Cuban creation – hey, it features rum... what did you expect? – the El Presidente was supposedly created by American bartender Eddie Woelke at the Jockey Club in Havana. Depending on who you believe, it was named after either President Mario García Menocal or President Gerardo Machado, but it doesn't really matter. All you really need to know is that Trader Vic (*see* opposite) described this drink as the 'Martini of Cuba', and that sums it up perfectly.

GLASSWARE
Rocks

ICE
Cubes to stir, ice sphere to serve

GARNISH
Orange twist

SERVES 1

50ml (1¾fl oz) Plantation Grande Réserve 5yo rum
25ml (¾fl oz) Antica Formula
10ml (2 tsp) orange curaçao
1 dash of Angostura bitters

Add all the ingredients to a mixing glass with ice. Stir well, then strain into a chilled rocks glass containing an ice sphere. Garnish with an orange twist.

Bartender's Tip
The older the rum, the better the drink! El Presidente is a very complex cocktail and the rum you use can make or break it.

Vic's Mai Tai

'There's been a lot of conversation over the beginning of the Mai Tai. And I want to set the record straight,' said legendary cocktail king Victor 'Trader Vic' Bergeron before he died. 'I originated the Mai Tai. Many others have claimed credit. All this aggravates my ulcer completely. Anyone who says I didn't create this drink is a dirty stinker.' That's settled then! This version is just as Vic intended, served short on the rocks.

GLASSWARE
Rocks

ICE
Cubes to shake and to serve

GARNISH
Mint sprig, orange slice, fresh cherry

SERVES 1

50ml (1¾fl oz) Plantation Grande Réserve 5yo rum
15ml (½fl oz) orange curaçao
25ml (¾fl oz) lime juice
15ml (½fl oz) Monin orgeat syrup

Add all the ingredients to a shaker with ice. Shake, then strain into a chilled rocks glass over ice. Garnish with a sprig of mint, an orange slice and a cherry.

Bartender's Tip
To give Vic's Mai Tai an added depth of flavour, combine dark and white rum (25ml/³/₄fl oz of each).

Scorpion

The Scorpion is another of Trader Vic's famous Tiki concoctions, but a definitive recipe there is not. In fact, Vic came up with three variations himself, and there are countless cover versions other bartenders have released. As a Tiki drink, most examples you will find serve the Scorpion long and over ice (or even longer in a Scorpion Bowl), but this slightly more sophisticated celebration of the non-negotiable mix of rum, brandy and citrus, sweetened with a lick of almond syrup, is served straight up.

GLASSWARE
Coupe

ICE
Cubes to shake, none to serve

GARNISH
Lime or orange twist

SERVES 1

35ml (1fl oz) Plantation Grande Réserve 5yo rum
15ml (½fl oz) Monin orgeat syrup
15ml (½fl oz) lemon juice
15ml (½fl oz) Hennessey Fine de Cognac
15ml (½fl oz) orange juice
1 dash of orange bitters

Bartender's Tip
Don't even think about not using freshly squeezed juice in the Scorpion. If you don't, the ghost of Trader Vic himself will come and haunt you!

Add all the ingredients to a shaker with ice. Shake, then strain into a chilled coupe glass and garnish with a lime or orange twist.

Planter's Punch

The first known printed reference to Planter's Punch appeared in the 8 August 1908 edition of the *New York Times*:
'This recipe I give to thee, dear brother in the heat.
Take two of sour (lime let it be) to one and a half of sweet,
Of Old Jamaica pour three strong, and add four parts of weak.
Then mix and drink. I do no wrong – I know whereof I speak.'

In honour of its creator, Fred L Myers, use Myers's dark Jamaican rum as the base.

GLASSWARE
Rocks

ICE
Cubes to shake and to serve

GARNISH
Grated nutmeg, orange slice

SERVES 1

50ml (1¾fl oz) Myers's dark rum
25ml (¾fl oz) lemon juice
25ml (¾fl oz) orange juice
20ml (¾fl oz) sugar syrup

Add all the ingredients to a shaker with ice. Shake, then strain into a chilled rocks glass over ice. Garnish with grated nutmeg and an orange slice.

Bartender's Tip
To tweak this recipe, garnish with a dash or three of Angostura bitters on the surface of the drink.

It's Called A Pineapple Head

Although this drink had suffered a bit of an identity crisis, after many late nights of extensive research we think we have finally revealed its true nomenclature. For my take on a summer Tiki drink I use Plantation Overproof rum. This is a strong spirit, but it is freshened up with chunks of pineapple, sharp lemon juice, Canadian maple syrup in place of sugar syrup, and a kick of background spice from the ginger.

GLASSWARE
Hurricane

ICE
Cubes to shake, crushed to serve

GARNISH
Pineapple leaf, pineapple triangle

SERVES 1

50ml (1¾fl oz) Plantation
    Overproof rum
25ml (¾fl oz) lemon juice
15ml (½fl oz) maple syrup
1 thumbnail-sized piece of
    fresh root ginger
2 chunks of fresh pineapple
1 dash of orange bitters

Bartender's Tip
For a more sophisticated hit on the Pineapple Head, serve it straight up in a chilled coupette glass.

Add all the ingredients to a shaker with ice. Shake, then strain into a hurricane glass over crushed ice. Garnish with a pineapple leaf and a pineapple triangle.

Christmas Rum Sour

Sour cocktails date back to Jerry Thomas' *How To Mix Drinks* book from 1862. Often described as the godfather of American mixology, the Professor (as he was also called) describes the classic sour as a base spirit with lemon or lime juice, egg white and a sweetener. My version was a Christmas experiment that is simply too good not to drink throughout the year. Jingle bells all the way!

GLASSWARE
Coupe

ICE
Cubes to shake, none to serve

GARNISH
None

SERVES 1

50ml (1¾fl oz) Plantation Overproof rum
25ml (¾fl oz) lemon juice
15ml (½fl oz) sugar syrup
1 dash of egg white
1 dash of Angostura bitters

Bartender's Tip
This is another of those important rules: make sure the eggs you use are as fresh as possible. Also, for a nice foamy top, do a dry shake first (*see* page 219).

Add all the ingredients to a shaker with ice. Shake, then strain into a chilled coupe glass and add a dash of Angostura bitters.

Hemingway Daiquiri

Originally created for the legendary writer by Constantino Ribalaigua at the El Floridita bar in Havana, the story goes that the hard-drinking adventurer sampled a frozen daiquiri but suggested doubling the rum and ditching the sugar. Thus was born the Hemingway Daiquiri (or the 'Papa Doble'). As the great man himself once said: 'I drink to make other people more interesting.'

GLASSWARE
Coupette or Martini

ICE
Cubes to shake, none to serve

GARNISH
Grapefruit twist

Add all the ingredients to a shaker with ice. Shake, then strain into a chilled coupette or Martini glass and garnish with a grapefruit twist.

SERVES 1

50ml (1¾fl oz) Bacardi
   Superior rum
20ml (¾fl oz) lime juice
20ml (¾fl oz) sugar syrup
15ml (½fl oz) grapefruit juice
1 dash of grapefruit bitters

Bartender's Tip
For the authentic Hemingway Daiquiri, drop the sugar – though this is not for the faint-hearted or the sensitive of palate.

Rum & Sherry Cobbler

Back in the late 19th century, the original Sherry Cobbler was a drink described by US bartending legend Harry 'The Dean' Johnson as 'without doubt the most popular beverage in the country'. And in 1875, it also prompted Mark Twain to recall with pride the moment 'when I witnessed the spectacle of an Englishman ordering an American Sherry Cobbler of his own free will and accord'. This is our in-house twist on the famous Jerry Thomas classic, dialling down the sherry and making rum the star of this stunning libation.

GLASSWARE
Sherry

ICE
Cubes to shake, none to serve

GARNISH
Pineapple leaf, raspberry

SERVES 1

2 chunks of fresh pineapple
2 slices of orange
35ml (1fl oz) Plantation Grande
  Réserve 5yo rum
20ml (¾fl oz) lime juice
20ml (¾fl oz) sugar syrup
15ml (½fl oz) triple sec
15ml (½fl oz) La Ina fino sherry

Muddle the fruits in the bottom of a shaker, then add the remaining ingredients and ice cubes. Shake, then strain into a chilled sherry glass. Garnish with a pineapple leaf and a raspberry.

Bartender's Tip
For a more authentic cobbler, add a few berries (blackberries, raspberries, strawberries) at the muddling stage.

Daiquiry Mulata

Another classic Daiquiri drink credited to Constantino 'El Grande Constante' Ribalaigua at El Floridita, only this version requires a darker aged rum to mix with the white crème de cacao for that memorable 'mulata' colouring from which it takes its name.

GLASSWARE
Coupe

ICE
Cubes to shake, none to serve

GARNISH
Grated nutmeg

SERVES 1

50ml (1¾fl oz) Havana Club 7yo rum
25ml (¾fl oz) lime juice
15ml (½fl oz) sugar syrup
15ml (½fl oz) white crème de cacao

Add all the ingredients to a shaker with ice. Shake, then strain into a chilled coupe glass. Garnish with grated nutmeg.

Bartender's Tip
Instead of shaking this cocktail, try adding the ingredients to a blender with some crushed ice and blitz them. This will create a thicker, frothier Mulata.

Hurricane

Pat O'Brien's cocktail creation takes its name from the glass it is served in and is synonymous with the French Quarter of New Orleans where it was first shaken up. Supposedly dreamt up during World War II when whiskey was in such short supply that it was only made available to bars if they ordered multiple cases of rum (which was plentiful), O'Brien's beverage enabled him to shift excess stocks of his sugar-cane-based spirit.

GLASSWARE
Hurricane

ICE
Cubes to shake, crushed to serve

GARNISH
Passion fruit half

SERVES 1

3 chunks of fresh pineapple
35ml (1fl oz) Plantation Grande
 Réserve 5yo rum
30ml (1fl oz) pineapple syrup
25ml (¾fl oz) lime juice

Muddle the fruit in the bottom of a shaker, then add the remaining ingredients and ice cubes. Shake, then strain into a chilled hurricane glass over crushed ice. Garnish with half a passion fruit.

Bartender's Tip
For the classic Hurricane, swap out the pineapple juice for passion fruit liqueur, which will also give the drink a pinkish hue.

Nuclear Daiquiri

A very modern creation, the Nuclear Daiquiri exploded from the mind of Gregor de Gruyther at London's LAB Bar in 2005. Tragically, Gregor died suddenly in 2009, but his powerful cocktail lives on. This simplified version is not as green as Gregor's original, but it still packs an atomic punch.

GLASSWARE
Coupe

ICE
Cubes to shake, none to serve

GARNISH
Lime twist

SERVES 1

50ml (1¾fl oz) Gosling's Overproof rum
25ml (¾fl oz) sugar syrup
25ml (¾fl oz) lime juice

Add all the ingredients to a shaker with ice. Shake, then strain into a chilled coupe glass. Garnish with a lime twist.

Bartender's Tip
For the original Nuclear Daiquiri, lose the sugar syrup and replace with 25ml (³⁄4fl oz) of green Chartreuse and 10ml (2 tsp) of Falernum syrup.

TEQUILA

'Tequila. Straight. There's a real polite drink. You keep drinking until you finally take one more and it just won't go down. Then you know you've reached your limit.'
Lee Marvin

Recipes by Francesco Turro Turrini

Lanes Of London

Tequila
by Louise Donovan

Ritualistic, misunderstood and often blamed for that roaring morning-after hangover, tequila hasn't always had the best reputation. But the spirit once associated with cowboys, bandits and Mexican outlaws has a lot more to offer than cheap shots washed down with a lick of salt and a mouthful of lime. Premium tequilas have risen steadily in stature over recent years and now take their rightful place alongside other fine spirits such as cognac and Scotch. Sure, some still mix lesser-quality tequila in Margaritas or prefer a neat down-in-one, but it has become the gauntlet for many bartenders, who challenge drinkers to sip rather than slam.

Even if tequila is perhaps not held in as high regard as its alcoholic brethren, it is among the most closely regulated spirits in the world, watched by the Mexican government and the Tequila Regulatory Council. Under Mexican law, all tequila must be made from the blue agave plant (*Agave tequilana*). Once the plant ripens (after roughly 8–12 years), the heart is removed, then cooked, and the sappy by-product is fermented and distilled into tequila. The spirit has Denomination of Origin (rather like Champagne or Brie cheese), which means it can be produced only in five Mexican states. Most is done in the state of Jalisco.

Tequila comes in two types: 100 per cent agave and *mixto*. For good tequila, always look for 100 per cent on the label: all the alcohol is fermented from the agave. *Mixto*, on the other hand, is at least 51 per cent agave tequila, as it has been blended with water and sugar; that means that if you drink *mixto*, you are mixing alcohols, which would account for the sore head. And where the notes in 100 per cent agave are robust and exotic, giving tequila its familiar spicy, earthy taste, *mixto* is subtler.

The ageing process helps 100 per cent agave tequilas to pack in more unique flavours. There are several types:
• *Joven* ('young'), also known as *oro* ('gold'), is freshly distilled and not aged at all, while *blanco* ('white'), also called *plata* ('silver'), is aged for less than two months. These have the strongest agave flavour (which is why most people shoot them).
• *Reposado* ('rested'), must age for at least two months, allowing the tequila to develop smooth, rich qualities. This makes it an ideal ingredient in a cocktail if you want the unique flavour of tequila without overpowering the rest of the drink.
• *Añejo* ('aged') is aged for a year or more, which contributes notes such as vanilla, crème brûlée, chocolate and oak. If it is aged for more than three years, it's often labelled *extra añejo*.

Adam Ennis, of Promixo Spirits UK, works with the direct descendants of the family who have owned Jose Cuervo tequila since 1795 and thinks it is the outsider nature of the drink that makes it so popular. 'Tequila is one of those where you think its going to be a bit of challenge, but nine times out of ten you can win people over,' he says. 'The drink is adaptable to all cocktails. From your Martini styles to drinks served long where certain spirits might get lost, tequila can come into its own.'

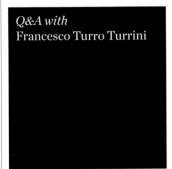

How did you get into the business? I used to work back of house in a diner when, during a busy weekend, one of the bartenders cut himself very badly and I was drafted in last minute to help. It was my first experience working behind the bar and I have never looked back. I realized I had a real passion for mixology and that my heart was firmly behind the bar, cocktail shaker in hand.

What is your bartending philosophy? I believe in taking your job seriously – but not yourself. Great chat coupled with a fast and tasty gin and tonic is undoubtedly the best bar experience. We are artists, not surgeons; so laugh often, especially with your guests.

What is the key to making a great cocktail? Use your knowledge to understand your guest. Don't shy away from asking questions, and ultimately don't make what is good for you – make something that can match the guest's taste.

Three great all-rounder tequilas recommended by Francesco Turro Turrini

1 Jose Cuervo Tradicional reposado
2 1800 reposado
3 Jose Cuervo Reserva de la Familia

As North America's first distilled drink and its first commercially produced alcohol, tequila is as rich in history as in flavours. Its roots reach back into pre-Hispanic times, when the natives fermented sap from the local maguey plants into a drink called *pulque*. (The heart, or *piña*, of maguey is today used to produce mezcal, and it is a bottle of mezcal, not tequila, that may sometimes contain a worm – a marketing gimmick that began in the 1940s.) *Pulque* first made its way into the United States in the late 19th century, as railroad transportation expanded. In the 20th century, its rise in popularity came down to two things. With Mexico just across the border, tequila became the drink of choice in the Southwest during Prohibition (1920–33). Then, during World War II, demand rose throughout the USA after spirits from Europe became harder to obtain.

Once limited to belt-pouring shot girls weeding you out of your money with overpriced slams, the image of tequila has also gone through a drastic transformation. Now it is not uncommon for a bar to offer a hundred-plus different bottles of tequila, with prices up to £275 for a single serving. Carlos Londoño, bar manager of Café Pacifico, the first commercial Mexican establishment in the UK, is spearheading this change. 'We've always associated tequila as a sexy drink, one that's mystical and one that we unfortunately like to relate to getting us very drunk,' he says. 'So at Café Pacifico we try to promote a different perception: we don't serve it in a shot glass, but in a serve glass, almost like a port or small wine glass. And we don't promote the salt and lime, or tequila girls.'

Add in the fact that George Clooney and Justin Timberlake are merely the latest in a long line of celebrity names associated with the drink, and you begin to get the picture. This rise of celebrity interest coincides with surging demand for the spirit. From 2002 to 2012, US imports of tequila soared 72 per cent, according to the Distilled Spirits Council of the United States. And what the US does, the UK follows – tequila's growth in the UK, at an average rate of 5.5 per cent per year, is outpacing nearly all rivals.

If you're still not convinced, tequila – believe it or not – even has some health benefits. In the 1930s, during an epidemic of Spanish influenza, doctors recommended a concoction of tequila, agave nectar and fresh lime juice to help fight off the illness. While we now have better remedies to fend off man flu, studies have shown that the spirit can break down dietary fat, which helps to lower cholesterol. Plus, the blue agave actually helps to promote calcium absorption and the regulation of lipid absorption, and can help fight diseases of the colon such as Crohn's disease, IBS and even cancer.

From the simple salt–lime combo to the rise of premium 100 per cent agave, tequila is having its well-earned moment. But whether you prefer to sip it alongside a homemade Sangrita, or mix up the classic G&T with tequila and tonic, or simply enjoy a free-flowing Margarita, there hasn't been a better time to drink Mexico's most famous export.

Margarita

There are many people who claim to have invented the Margarita; as Spanish for 'daisy' and a popular woman's name, it would have been a common name for a drink. This is my favourite story: the cocktail was created in the Rancho La Gloria bar near Rosarito, Mexico, by Carlos 'Danny' Herrera, for an actress/showgirl named Marjorie King, who would drink no spirit but tequila. The iconic salt rim was added, alongside Cointreau and freshly squeezed lime juice, and Herrera named the drink after Marjorie.

GLASSWARE
Rocks

ICE
Cubes to shake, none to serve

GARNISH
Sea salt, lime slice

SERVES 1

50ml (1¾fl oz) Jose Cuervo
Tradicional reposado tequila
20ml (¾fl oz) lime juice
25ml (¾fl oz) curaçao or
Cointreau
Sea salt

Coat the rim of a chilled rocks glass in some lime juice from the lime slice garnish, then dip the rim into the salt ensuring it is coated evenly. Add all the ingredients to a shaker with ice. Shake, then strain the cocktail into the glass being careful not to touch the edge of the glass. Garnish with the lime slice.

Bartender's Tip
Make sure the salt remains on the outside of the rim and doesn't dissolve into the drink (if you can avoid it).

El Diablo

This devilish drink originated in California during the Forties – the oldest known recipe is in *Trader Vic's Book of Food & Drink*, published in 1946. A long and refreshing cocktail, it benefits from the sweetness of the cassis offsetting the tequila and the spiciness of the ginger ale. Don't forget to serve with a straw.

GLASSWARE
Collins

ICE
Cubes to shake and to serve

GARNISH
Lime husk or half a lime shell, pomegranate seeds

SERVES 1

50ml (1¾fl oz) Gran Centenario reposado tequila
20ml (¾fl oz) lime juice
15ml (½fl oz) crème de cassis
10ml (2 tsp) homemade ginger syrup (*see* Bartender's Tip)
Ginger ale, to top up

Add all the ingredients except the ginger ale to a shaker with ice. Shake, then strain into a chilled Collins glass over ice. Top up with ginger ale and stir. Garnish with a lime husk or half a lime shell and a few pomegranate seeds.

Bartender's Tip
Don't use an artificial ginger syrup as it will make the drink too sweet and not spicy enough. If you can't make your own, peel a thumbnail-sized piece of fresh root ginger and shake it with the ingredients.

Tommy's Margarita

Tommy's Margarita was created by mixology legend Julio Bermejo and named after the eponymous San Francisco-based Mexican bar and restaurant. Julio stocks more than 400 tequilas in his bar, and is nothing short of a Margarita maestro. Lacking the traditional orange liqueur, it is the agave notes in Tommy's Margarita that make it distinctive. It is also worth noting that Julio serves it without salt so as not to ruin the taste of the tequila.

GLASSWARE
Martini

ICE
Cubes to shake, none to serve

GARNISH
Lime wedge

SERVES 1

50ml (1¾fl oz) Jose Cuervo Tradicional reposado tequila
20ml (¾fl oz) lime juice
25ml (¾fl oz) Agave Water (*see* Bartender's Tip)

Bartender's Tip
To make agave water: cut the nectar (or buy it in a squeezy bottle) and blend 2 parts nectar with 1 part water at room temperature – let it set and blend without heating or stirring. Store in the refrigerator.

Add all the ingredients to a shaker with ice. Shake, then strain into a chilled Martini glass. Garnish with a lime wedge.

Toreador

A beautifully simple recipe, details of the Toreador were first published in 1937 in William J Tarling's *Café Royal Cocktail Book*, which was one of the earliest publications to mention tequila-based drinks. As well as the Toreador, Tarling also presented a recipe for a cocktail he called the Picador – a British version of the cocktail that would appear in the US as the Margarita 16 years later. Make of that what you will! The Toreador differs from the Picador (and by extension the Margarita) by swapping apricot brandy for triple sec.

GLASSWARE
Coupe or Martini

ICE
Cubes to shake, none to serve

GARNISH
Lemon twist

SERVES 1

50ml (1¾fl oz) 1800 reposado tequila
20ml (¾fl oz) lime juice
25ml (¾fl oz) apricot brandy

Add all the ingredients to a shaker with ice. Shake, then strain into a chilled coupe or Martini glass. Garnish with a lemon twist.

Bartender's Tip
Feel free to add a dash of sugar if you find this drink too sour – a teaspoon of caster sugar will make a big difference.

Matador

Another gem from the *Café Royal Cocktail Book*, this cocktail is a fierce and fiery drop for the bold imbiber. With the vermouth matching the tequila, the Matador is a Martini-style drink delivered with a lovely hint of orange. Drink more than three, though, and you might just feel like you've been hit by a bull the next morning!

GLASSWARE
Coupe

ICE
Cubes to throw, none to serve

GARNISH
Orange twist

SERVES 1

30ml (1fl oz) Jose Cuervo Platino tequila
30ml (1fl oz) dry vermouth
30ml (1fl oz) curaçao

Add all the ingredients to a shaker with ice. Mix using the throw style (*see* page 219) until chilled (if you are not comfortable with this style of mixing, a long stir would work as well), then strain into a chilled coupe glass. Garnish with a fancy orange twist.

Bartender's Tip
Make sure the vermouth is fresh, not from an old bottle that has been languishing on a shelf for years. Once opened, keep vermouth in a refrigerator; if you don't use it very often, buy a small-sized bottle.

Bloody Maria

The true origin of the Bloody Mary is disputed, but it is generally believed to have been created by Fernand Petiot (*see* page 35). However, what is certain is that by swapping tequila for vodka, Mary becomes Maria. Another hard fact, as far as I am concerned, is that this classic brunch cocktail is the best hangover cure there is.

GLASSWARE
Collins

ICE
Cubes to throw and serve

GARNISH
Lemon wedge, cherry tomato, celery ribbon, salt, pepper

SERVES 1

50ml (1¾fl oz) 1800 reposado tequila
120ml (4fl oz) tomato juice
10ml (2 tsp) lemon juice
5ml (1 tsp) Agave Water (*see* Bartender's Tip on page 79)
8 drops of Tabasco hot pepper sauce
4 dashes of Worcestershire sauce
2 pinches of celery salt
2 grinds of black pepper
10ml (2 tsp) mezcal

Add all the ingredients except the mezcal to a shaker with ice. Mix using the throw style (or a long stir) until chilled (*see* page 219). Strain into a chilled Collins glass over ice. Float the mezcal on top, then garnish with a lemon wedge, a cherry tomato, a celery ribbon and salt and pepper to taste.

Bartender's Tip
A dash of sweet will enhance the flavour and balance the acidity of the tomato juice. If you don't have agave water, sugar will do just as well.

Silk Stocking

The Silk Stocking was once a very popular dessert Martini. If you are a fan of fruity, creamy cocktails, you will really like this one. The hints of the sweet darkness of chocolate and pomegranate are backed by tequila to keep things interesting.

GLASSWARE
Coupe

ICE
Cubes to stir, none to serve

GARNISH
Dark chocolate powder

SERVES 1

50ml (1¾fl oz) 1800 añejo tequila
20ml (¾fl oz) white crème de cacao
20ml (¾fl oz) double cream
5ml (1 tsp) pomegranate syrup

Add all the ingredients to a shaker with ice. Stir, then strain into a chilled coupe glass. Garnish with a dusting of dark chocolate powder.

Bartender's Tip
Be careful when you measure the cream as too much can mask the delicate flavour of this amazing drink.

Rosita

This twist on the famous Negroni appears in a 1988 edition of *Mr Boston Official Bartender's Guide*. It was rediscovered by Gary Regan in 1991 in *The Bartender's Bible*, but he had added a typical 'Gaz' touch: namely a dash of bitters and, predictably, a bit more tequila. For my own version, I tinkered with the proportions and dropped the dry vermouth and I think it does the job.

GLASSWARE
Rocks

ICE
Cubes to stir, none to serve

GARNISH
Lemon twist, orange slice

SERVES 1

30ml (1fl oz) Gran Centenario plata tequila
30ml (1fl oz) Punt e Mes
30ml (1fl oz) Campari
1 dash of Angostura bitters

Add all the ingredients to a mixing glass with ice and stir until diluted to your taste. Strain and pour into the rocks glass. Garnish with a fancy lemon twist and an orange slice.

Bartender's Tip
The Punt e Mes can be replaced with a sweet vermouth. If still you find the drink too bitter, omit the Angostura bitters and add an extra 5ml (1 tsp) of the sweet vermouth.

Love In Jalisco

This cocktail was one of the first times I ever mixed with tequila. Love in Jalisco has had many facelifts over the years, but it now has a rich peach flavour and dry saltiness with a backbone of tequila that is strengthened by the absinthe, all of which creates a balanced rather than dry or sweet flavour. This is a serious cocktail with serious repercussions for the overindulgent.

GLASSWARE
Wine

ICE
Cubes to stir, clear block to serve

GARNISH
Luxardo maraschino cherry soaked in absinthe

SERVES 1

50ml (1¾fl oz) Maestro Dobel tequila
20ml (¾fl oz) Tio Pepe sherry
25ml (¾fl oz) peach brandy
5 dashes of absinthe

Bartender's Tip
Be very careful with the absinthe as it can easily overpower any drink.

Add all the ingredients to a mixing glass with ice and stir. Strain over a clear block of ice into the glass. Garnish with a maraschino cherry that has been soaked in absinthe.

Clever Club

I read once that tequila makes you smarter. The name of this cocktail is therefore a twist on the original Clover Club recipe from 1909 in *Drinks - How to Mix and How to Serve* by Paul E Lowe. In the original recipe the lemon juice is omitted, but this is thought to be a mistake. In this version the sweetness from the syrup plays nicely against the dry and nutty silver tequila.

GLASSWARE
Coupe or coupette

ICE
Cubes to shake, none to serve

GARNISH
3 raspberries

SERVES 1

50ml (1¾fl oz) 1800 silver tequila
20ml (¾fl oz) lime juice
20ml (¾fl oz) sugar syrup
20ml (¾fl oz) egg white
3 raspberries

Add all the ingredients to a shaker (without ice) and dry shake, briefly, but vigorously (*see* page 219). Add ice and shake again, then strain into a chilled coupe or coupette glass. Garnish by tossing the raspberries on to the velvety foam surface of the drink.

Bartender's Tip
The key for this cocktail is a very good dry shake and fresh raspberries. No syrup can deliver the same flavour as fresh fruit.

Mexican Gland

People often ask me to impress the lady sat next to them. My response is a twist on an old classic, the Monkey Gland, created by Harry MacElhone at his bar in Paris. Swapping the original gin for a shot of tequila gives it a feisty boost.

GLASSWARE
Martini or coupe

ICE
Cubes to stir, none to serve

GARNISH
Ground cinnamon

SERVES 1

40ml (1¼fl oz) Gran Centenario plata tequila
40ml (1¼fl oz) orange juice
5ml (1 tsp) pomegranate syrup
3 dashes of absinthe

Dip the rim of a chilled Martini or coupe glass into the cinnamon ensuring it is coated evenly. Add all the ingredients to a mixing glass with ice and stir. Strain into the Martini or coupe to serve.

Bartender's Tip
Make sure you use freshly squeezed orange juice – half an orange will be more than enough.

Tequila Gibson

Ask for a Gibson and you will earn every bartender's respect: ask for one with tequila and you will be his favourite guest. This cocktail comes with drinking instructions:

1. Have a sip and eat one onion
2. There are five onions so drink it in five sips
3. Don't drink more than five... Trust me!

GLASSWARE
Martini, shot

ICE
Cubes to stir, none to serve

GARNISH
5 cocktail onions

SERVES 1

60ml (2fl oz) 1800 silver tequila
10ml (2 tsp) manzanilla sherry

Add all the ingredients to a mixing glass with ice and stir. Strain into a chilled Martini glass. Serve with cocktail onions in a shot glass on the side.

Bartender's Tip
Just to reiterate...
No. More. Than. Five.
You'll thank me in
the morning.

Royal Paloma

This cocktail is inspired by a cocktail well known in Mexico – La Paloma – which was created by the legendary Don Javier Delgado Corona, owner/bartender of La Capilla (The Chapel) in Tequila. My interpretation drops soda in favour of decadent and delicious champagne, which really gives this cocktail a royal seal of approval.

GLASSWARE
Flute

ICE
Cubes to shake, none to serve

GARNISH
Luxardo maraschino cherry, orange twist

SERVES 1

15ml (½fl oz) Jose Cuervo
    Tradicional reposado tequila
20ml (¾fl oz) pink grapefruit
    juice
15ml (½fl oz) Luxardo
    maraschino liqueur
10ml (2 tsp) agave water
    (*see* Bartender's Tip on page 79)
Champagne, to top up

Bartender's Tip
This is the perfect drink to be made in pitchers on a hot day. Multiply everything by six and top up with a bottle of champagne. Enjoy it with friends.

Add all the ingredients except the champagne to a shaker with ice. Shake, then strain into a chilled flute and top up with champagne. Drop a maraschino cherry into the glass and garnish with an orange twist.

L' Jefe

This drink was created by Davide Segat in honour of the much-loved Henry Besant, who made tequila his passion and his life. By writing about tequila here, I am also honouring Besant's work and research to prove to the world that tequila is not simply a shot for hedonistic twentysomethings, but a true spirit that deserves respect.

GLASSWARE
Wine

ICE
Cubes to shake, none to serve

GARNISH
Grated tonka beans

SERVES 1

50ml (1¾fl oz) Altos plata tequila
25ml (¾fl oz) lime juice
25ml (¾fl oz) tamarind and pale ale reduction (*see* Bartender's Tip)
3 dashes of Del Maguey Minero mezcal

Add all the ingredients to a shaker with ice. Shake, then strain into a chilled wine glass. Garnish with a sprinkle of grated tonka beans.

Bartender's Tip
The pale ale reduction is pretty easy to make: boil 250ml (8fl oz) of your favourite pale ale in a small saucepan with 50g (2oz) tamarind paste. Simmer until reduced by a third, let it cool and store it in a sealed bottle in the fridge.

T.B.C.
(Tequila Beer Chaser)

As with most of the cool things in life, there is always a 'to be continued'. If you have managed to drink all of the previous tequila cocktails (not in one session, please!), you are probably ready to sit down and enjoy a good tequila chased by a good beer.

GLASSWARE
Beer, sherry

ICE
None

GARNISH
None

SERVES 1

330ml (11fl oz) Meantime wheat beer
50ml (1¾fl oz) Jose Cuervo Reserva de la Familia tequila

Bartender's Tip
Enjoy slowly, but don't let the beer warm up too much.

Pour the cold beer into a chilled beer glass and let it stand for a moment. Pour the tequila into a nice tasting glass, such as a sherry glass, and have a sip. Refresh your mouth with the beer and keep going back and forth between the two drinks.

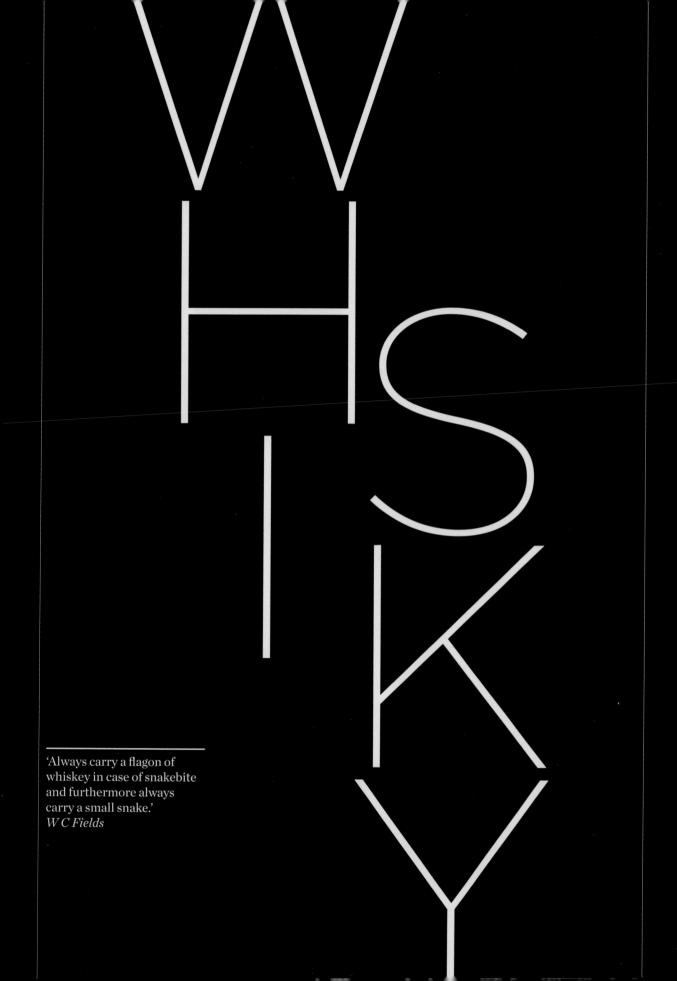

'Always carry a flagon of whiskey in case of snakebite and furthermore always carry a small snake.'
W C Fields

Recipes by Scott Green

34 Grosvenor Square, London

Whisky
by Alex Godfrey

In *The Gonzo Papers, Vol. 2: Generation of Swine: Tales of Shame and Degradation in the '80s*, Hunter S Thompson stated: 'Maybe this is all pure gibberish – a product of the demented imagination of a lazy drunken hillbilly with a heart full of hate who has found a way to live out where the real winds blow – to sleep late, have fun, get wild, drink whiskey, and drive fast on empty streets with nothing in mind except falling in love and not getting arrested... *Res ipsa loquitur*. Let the good times roll.'

Hunter S Thompson knew how to drink. Whisky has set many a soul on fire: from moonshine to Manhattans, it has inspired us for centuries. If you go back far enough, it was called the water of life, or *aqua vitae*. You might think that *water* is the water of life, but not so according to the Gaels. The word 'whiskey' was first used in 12th-century Ireland, an anglicization of the Irish Gaelic *uisce* ('water'), which has its roots in the Scottish Gaelic *uisge beatha*: water of life. Italians of the 13th century were the first on record to get the party started by distilling alcohol, and whisky became all the rage soon after, when distilleries in Scotland and Ireland, short on grapes, began working with barley grain. The drink found fame in 1405 when, in the Irish Annals of Clonmacnoise, it was given as the cause of death of a chieftain who apparently consumed 'a surfeit of aqua vitae' at Christmas. So much for the water of life, eh chieftain?

The Scots popularized it at around the same time (James IV of Scotland was a big fan), and they had mastered the art by the 19th century, creating the first blended whisky (Andrew Usher's Old Vatted Glenlivet) in 1853. The whisky/whiskey divide dates back to about that time; when the Irish exported their own distilled elixir to America, they added an 'e' in order to differentiate it from Scottish whisky, which they were also exporting. The 'e' has also often been used for those distilled in the US. However, inconsistencies abound and today the spelling differentiation is all but redundant.

Prohibition, ironically but predictably, was responsible for a seismic surge in the drink's popularity in the USA during the 1920s and early '30s. Because alcohol was banned for anything other than medicinal purposes, wily doctors began writing liquor prescriptions and, soon enough, pharmacy shelves were stacked high with whiskey. The water of life: just what the doctor ordered, indeed. Keep guzzling those hot toddies, folks. (Walgreens, in fact, saw their number of stores grow from 20 to 397 in the 1920s alone, and their position today as America's largest drug-retailing chain has whiskey to thank.)

Whether it's malt (from malted barley) or grain (from, well, grains), the right whisky will find you. The smoky tones of Scotch come from peat fires. It is generally distilled twice, and Irish whiskey thrice. Jack Daniel's whiskey ('nectar of the gods', according to Frank Sinatra, who was buried with a bottle of the stuff) is mellowed through 10 feet (3 meters) of hard sugar maple charcoal. In 1964, the US Congress officially declared bourbon 'a distinctive product of the United States', and rock 'n' roll clasped it to its pierced bosom. The likes of Keith Richards and Slash became synonymous with Jack Daniel's (although, due to the brand's aforementioned filtering process, it likes

How did you get into the business? I literally took the first job I found after school in a hotel bar in Dorset. A charming colleague told me that I should start reading the backs of the bottles because I might find them interesting. Ten years later and I'm writing the blurb on the backs of bottles myself.

Who was your mentor/bartending inspiration? I've had many, from the guy who was running the first bar I worked in, in London, who taught (whether rightly or wrongly) that drinks take second place to ambience, consistency and the customer interaction, to the bartenders, master distillers, winemakers and even baristas who have blown my socks off with their creativity and originality.

What is your favourite bar in the world? I've never been let down by Artesian at The Langham, The Connaught Bar or The American Bar at The Savoy. I don't have the guts to choose one out of the three...utter genius just drips from the woodwork in those places.

Three great all-rounder whiskies recommended by Scott Green

1 Lagavulin 16yo
   malt whisky
2 Glenfarclas 15yo
   malt whisky
3 Woodford Reserve
   bourbon

to differentiate itself from bourbon), and the association with rock stars continues. In 2009's 'TiK ToK', Ke$ha sang that she brushed her teeth 'with a bottle of Jack', although we presume she means the contents of the bottle, and in any case she's probably lying. But still.

The Sunset Strip's Whisky a Go Go nightclub still thrives on its debauched 1970s reputation, and whiskey is a mainstay of popular culture. Bill Murray, in the film *Lost in Translation*, introduced the world to Japan's Suntory (which in January 2014 bought the US bourbon company Jim Beam for $16 billion). Ron Burgundy, of *Anchorman* fame, loves his 'Scotchy Scotch Scotch' (which inspired the Ben & Jerry's ice cream of the same name), while in Quentin Tarantino's film *Inglourious Basterds*, Brad Pitt's character, Aldo Raine, wears his bootlegging as a badge of honour: 'A man just trying to earn a living for his family selling moonshine liquor.' As dangerous as it is, moonshine still thrives in the USA today, especially in Appalachia, and the exploits of some of its practitioners are currently documented on The Discovery Channel's reality show *Moonshiners*, which, according to suppliers, has seen a huge upsurge in sales of fermenting yeast and stills.

Indeed, whisky's overall popularity is growing, and the industry is constantly adapting to keep up. Alex Huskinson, manager of The Whisky Exchange's London store, has worked there for six years, and says that within those six years 'the whole whisky industry has changed dramatically. It's gone from being a relatively niche product to being very popular, very fashionable. Young people are starting to get more interested; more women are interested in it. The whole whisky investment side has exploded. Whisky was seen as cool in the 1950s, but back then, cool people were older men. The TV series *Mad Men* has helped, but that's by the by – youth culture is much more prevalent now and young people have started to see whisky as a desirable thing to be into. Really, though, whisky is just nice! And more people are noticing. Japanese whisky is doing really well, and among the Scotches, Islay whisky – the smoky stuff – is becoming very popular.'

Scotch whisky, in fact, accounts for a quarter of all UK food and drink exports and, according to Scottish Rural Affairs and Environment Secretary Richard Lochhead, earns £135 a second there. Across the board, new recipes are appearing with great frequency. Honey whisky, very pleasurable on the taste buds, is on the rise, and whisky cocktails are ever desirable. Water of life? Well, the Old Fashioned started life as a 'hair of the dog' hangover saviour, and the Whisky Sour was used to fight off scurvy. Maybe it is not such a stretch after all. That Hunter S Thompson knew a good thing when he drank it.

Sweet Manhattan

Manhattans can be served either sweet, dry (made with white vermouth and whiskey) or perfect (equal parts vermouth and whiskey). In my opinion, sweet tastes the best – the red vermouth's bitter-sweetness results in a complex, understated drink. Supposedly, the Manhattan was invented at the Manhattan Club in New York for Lady Randolph Churchill (mother to the late Sir Winston). Different recipes alternate between rye whiskey and bourbon. The original recipe is with rye, and I like to keep it this way. Bourbon is too sweet for me. The dryness, herbal nuttiness and spiciness of rye works well with the vermouth.

GLASSWARE
Martini

ICE
Cubes to stir, none to serve

GARNISH
Fresh cherry (or a Luzardo maraschino cherry if fresh are not in season)

SERVES 1

50ml (1¾fl oz) Rittenhouse Straight Rye 100 proof whiskey
25ml (¾fl oz) Antica Formula red vermouth
2 dashes of The Bitter Truth Old Time aromatic bitters

Add all the ingredients to a chilled mixing glass with ice and stir until diluted to your taste and ice-cold. Strain into a chilled Martini glass and garnish with a cherry.

Bartender's Tip
Watch out: the balance between the whiskey and vermouth flavours is easy to ruin here. Trial and error in accordance with your personal tastes will get you the best results, rather than steadfastly following a recipe.

Old Fashioned

One of the earliest mentions of the 'cock-tail' comes from Jerry Thomas, the American godfather of mixed drinks, describing it as a 'stimulating liquor, composed of spirits of any kind, sugar, water and bitters'. This concoction is what we now know as an Old Fashioned, albeit slightly modified as it's been handed down over the years. The method of making an Old Fashioned is subject to an enormous amount of debate. In my opinion, adding either soda or water is passé. The bitters and the sugar are there to complement the spirit, not mask it: this drink is essentially perfect as is and should be kept as simple as possible.

GLASSWARE
Rocks

ICE
Cubes to stir and to serve

GARNISH
Orange twist

SERVES 1

50ml (1¾fl oz) Eagle Rare bourbon
15ml (½fl oz) sugar syrup
2 dashes of Angostura bitters

Fill a chilled mixing glass with ice. Add the bourbon and sugar syrup, then two dashes of bitters (with bitters, too little is better than too much – you can add more to taste later if two dashes is not enough). Stir until chilled and diluted to your taste. Strain into a chilled rocks glass over ice. Zest a generous twist of orange to release the oils over the drink (*see* page 219), then use to garnish.

Bartender's Tip
Try a dash or two of peach bitters in any bourbon cocktail. Never fails.

Mint Julep

The julep was originally a Persian drink called a *gulab*, which means rosewater. The julep made its way to Europe, where the rose petals of the original drink were replaced by easier-to-find mint leaves. However, the Mint Julep is mostly famous for being the official drink of the Kentucky Derby, which produces hundreds of thousands of juleps every year for the official event. Original recipes would have contained either Cognac, rum or whiskey, the latter eventually becoming the connoisseur's choice. A julep tin is as iconic as the drink itself, but if you find yourself without one, you can easily substitute a rocks glass.

GLASSWARE
Julep tin or rocks

ICE
Crushed ice to stir and to serve

GARNISH
Mint sprig

10 fresh mint leaves
15ml (½fl oz) sugar syrup
2 dashes of Angostura bitters
50ml (1¾fl oz) Four Roses
  bourbon

Squeeze 10 or so mint leaves in the palms of your hands (as if you were clapping) to release their natural oils and flavour. After squeezing, drop the leaves in the bottom of a julep tin or rocks glass. Add the sugar syrup and bitters. Fill the tin or glass with crushed ice and add the bourbon. Stir for longer than you would imagine – the dilution and flavour of the mint will become more prominent the more you stir. Top up with more crushed ice and garnish with an attractive sprig of mint.

Bartender's Tip
The potential sin here is muddling the mint – that is, crushing the leaves and releasing bitter drink-destroying flavours. A firm rub or a squeeze between your palms will release all the minty goodness you will need.

Blood & Sand

This cocktail was named after the 1922 film *Blood and Sand,* starring Rudolph Valentino. A deliciously off-dry version was included in Harry Craddock's *The Savoy Cocktail Book,* published in 1930. Where some cocktails are designed to celebrate the base spirit, the Blood & Sand is about the balance of all four ingredients. For that reason, I chose Oban malt whisky for its uniqueness – the discerning drinker will notice the new dimensions that the Oban adds, most noticeably with its characteristic gentle peatiness and lack of the medicinal sea influences of the neighbouring island malts.

GLASSWARE
Coupe or Martini

ICE
Cubes to shake, none to serve

GARNISH
Fresh cherry

Add all the ingredients to a shaker with ice. Shake vigorously, then double strain (*see* page 219) into a chilled coupe or Martini glass. Garnish with a fresh cherry.

SERVES 1

20ml (¾fl oz) Oban 1996 The Distiller's Edition whisky
20ml (¾fl oz) Cocchi Rosso red vermouth
20ml (¾fl oz) Cherry Heering liqueur
20ml (¾fl oz) orange juice

Bartender's Tip
Shake this drink as hard as you can before your arms give out to achieve a truly unsurpassable texture. And because this drink has a tendency to be on the sweet side, a clandestine dash or two of aromatic bitters can help the balance a little.

Rob Roy

Invented by a New York City bartender in 1894, the Rob Roy is essentially a Sweet Manhattan upgraded with Scotch. It has a rich pedigree: the drink was created for an opera called 'Rob Roy' by Hector Berlioz, which was in turn inspired by Sir Walter Scott's novel *Rob Roy*, which was about Scottish folk hero Robert Roy MacGregor. The drink benefits greatly from the Scotch, which provides a lot of character, individuality and flavour. This means that your choice of Scotch and vermouth is incredibly important – the quality of the spirit will have a direct and noticeable impact on the quality of the drink.

GLASSWARE
Martini

ICE
Cubes to stir, none to serve

GARNISH
Fresh cherry

SERVES 1

50ml (1¾fl oz) Highland Park 18yo Scotch whisky
25ml (¾fl oz) Antica Formula red vermouth
2 dashes of The Bitter Truth Old Time aromatic bitters

Add all the ingredients to a chilled mixing glass with ice and stir until diluted to your taste and ice-cold. Strain into a chilled Martini glass and garnish with a fresh cherry.

Bartender's Tip
Balance is key, and best results will come from experimenting with quantities on your own. If you like a Rob Roy that is heavier on vermouth, feel free to nudge the amount up to 30ml or even 35ml (1fl oz).

Thomas H. Handy Sazerac

Created around 1850 by Aaron Bird in the Sazerac Coffee House in New Orleans, the recipe was originally Sazerac de Forge et Fils Cognac, absinthe, sugar and Peychaud's bitters (Antoine Peychaud was a local chemist). After the phylloxera epidemic that devastated 90 per cent of wine and brandy production in Europe, one Thomas H. Handy took over as owner of the coffee house, and due to shortages of Cognac, began serving the Sazerac cocktail with American rye whiskey. The recipe stuck. This is a recipe created in homage to him, but be forewarned: the whiskey is 64.2% ABV, so dilute accordingly.

GLASSWARE
Rocks

ICE
Cubes to stir, none to serve

GARNISH
Lemon twist

SERVES 1

50ml (1¾fl oz) Sazerac Thomas H. Handy Straight Rye whiskey
15ml (½fl oz) sugar syrup
2 dashes of Peychaud's bitters
1 dash of Jade 1901 absinthe

Add all the ingredients to a chilled mixing glass with ice. With absinthe, just like bitters, less is more: if you find a dash or two of each is not enough, you can always add more later. Stir the cocktail until diluted to your taste and ice-cold. Strain into a chilled rocks glass and garnish with a lemon twist.

Bartender's Tip
This one is slightly off-the-wall: keep your absinthe in a perfume atomizer. This will give it a perfect mist-in-the-glass quality without the laborious ritual of the in-and-out absinthe 'rinse'.

Whiskey Sour

According to 19th-century drink classifications, a sour is any drink with lemon juice and sugar. The inclusion of egg white technically makes this a Boston Sour, but most contemporary bars will make a sour with egg white as standard. It has a complicated blend of flavours, and is a great example of how important the balance of sweet and sour can be in a drink, as well as the delicate use of egg white. If it's made well, the Whiskey Sour is one of the single best cocktails in the world. If it's made badly, you'll remember it as one of the worst. Add a couple of dashes of absinthe to turn the Whiskey Sour into a Rattlesnake.

Add all the ingredients to a shaker (without ice) and dry shake briefly, but vigorously (*see* page 219), then add ice and shake again. (Do note that it's very easy to lose control of your shaker and spray your guests with egg white and bitters. Using a Parisian shaker is your best bet, but if that's not an option you can tightly wrap a tea towel around where the two parts of your shaker meet in order to prevent any spillage.) Double strain (*see* page 219) into a chilled rocks glass over ice and garnish with a lemon twist and a fresh cherry.

GLASSWARE
Rocks

ICE
Cubes to stir and to serve

GARNISH
Lemon twist, fresh cherry

SERVES 1

50ml (1¾fl oz) Hudson Baby Bourbon
20ml (¾fl oz) lemon juice
15ml (½fl oz) sugar syrup
⅔ egg white
2 dashes of Angostura bitters

Bartender's Tip
Keep an eye on the sweetness here. Bourbons can be deceptively sweet in comparison to Scotch or Japanese whisky and this drink, for me, is best when served just on the tart side.

Mizuwari

Mizuwari means 'mixed with water' in Japanese, but this isn't a simple Scotch & Soda. The Mizuwari is one of the best ways to enjoy Japan's burgeoning whisky offerings that are currently taking the world by storm. It's a great way to drink any style of Japanese whisky, which is typically lighter than Scotch but more complex and less sweet than bourbon. Due to the simplicity of this drink, quality is of the essence. This means high-quality water and high-quality ice. Although simple, the joy of a Mizuwari lies in the inimitable combination of taste and ritual.

GLASSWARE
Highball

ICE
Large cubes

GARNISH
None

SERVES 1

50ml (1¾fl oz) Hibiki 17yo whisky
Still spring water

This drink is defined by its method. Fill a chilled highball glass with the largest, cleanest ice cubes you can find or make. Very slowly pour over the Hibiki whisky and stir gently. Then, hold the stirring spoon over the centre of the glass, just above the rim, and slowly pour the spring water to taste over the back of the spoon (usually somewhere between 50–100ml/1¾–3½ fl oz). Stir gently until ice-cold and serve.

Bartender's Tip
Patience is key here. This is not a whisky and water – it's a Mizuwari. If you don't have the right ice, the right whisky and the most meticulous feel for dilution, then you don't have a Mizuwari!

Whisky Mac

The Whisky Mac is attributed to a certain Colonel MacDonald, who began adding ginger wine to his Scotch while serving in India during the days of the British Empire. If you don't drown it in the ginger wine, a Whisky Mac can be a nice alternative way to enjoy a good Scotch, despite its reputation as the drink of choice for the more mature. My advice would be to try to steer towards more fragrant and genteel Speyside or Lowland whiskies, as anything with too pronounced a flavour will clash with the ginger wine. This is a great winter drink, and can sometimes even be served warm with a touch of hot water as a toddy.

GLASSWARE
Martini

ICE
Cubes to stir, none to serve

GARNISH
None

SERVES 1

45ml (1½fl oz) Glenfarclas 15yo whisky
30ml (1fl oz) ginger wine

Add the Scotch and ginger wine to a chilled mixing glass with ice. Stir gently, then strain into a chilled Martini glass.

Bartender's Tip
Don't knock a Whisky Mac until you've tried it. If you add a drop or two of aromatic bitters, this is a fantastic alternative to an Old Fashioned.

San-Ju Yon

This cocktail is essentially a Far Eastern Mint Julep. Aojiso (or green shiso) is an Asian relative of common mint, stronger in flavour with more spice. Nikka From the Barrel pairs well with the strong savoury notes of the shiso leaf and the sweetness of the ginger cordial. Hermes is a rare brand of bitters made by Japanese drinks giant Suntory. Because the Japanese palate is typically much less receptive to heavy bitterness, Hermes is lighter and less astringent than other, more common brands, such as Angostura or Peychaud's. Should Hermes orange bitters be too difficult to source, feel free to replace with another brand.

GLASSWARE
Julep tin or rocks

ICE
Crushed ice to stir and to serve

GARNISH
Aojiso leaf, waka momo (Japanese baby peaches), star anise

SERVES 1

2 shiso leaves
1 tsp store bought or homemade ginger cordial (*see* below)
45ml (1½fl oz) Nikka From The Barrel whisky
15ml (½fl oz) plum sake liqueur
2 dashes of Hermes orange bitters

For the ginger cordial (makes 500ml)
25g (about 2cm/1in) fresh root ginger, peeled and finely diced
500ml (17fl oz) mineral water
750g (1½lb) caster sugar

Bartender's Tip
Be wary of the strong flavour of the aojiso leaves. If you agitate too much, they'll overpower the drink; not enough and they'll be a pointless contribution. My best advice is to tear the leaves in half only and avoid muddling.

First make the ginger cordial. Pour the mineral water into a shallow saucepan and bring to the boil, then add the ginger and sugar. Simmer over a medium heat for 7 minutes. Strain, then bottle in a sterilized container and refrigerate until needed.

To make the cocktail, tear the aojiso leaves in half and drop them into a chilled julep tin or rocks glass. Add ginger cordial, then the crushed ice almost to the brim. Add the remaining ingredients and stir vigorously. Top up with more crushed ice and garnish with an aojiso leaf, a waka momo and a star anise.

Happy In A Haze

An important element in what is essentially an augmented Scotch & Ginger is the specific variety of Talisker whisky. The 57° North is a non-chill-filtered expression of the infamous Skye malt, bottled at a higher ABV and with no colourant added. The bitters choice came about by an accident that a friend, Kat Mazaniova, had while trying to infuse gin: rather than adding a pinch of her signature blend of herbs to a gin, she added the entire bottle of gin to the entire batch of herbs. The result was an extremely small batch of highly concentrated, gin-based liquorice bitters. However, ordinary liquorice bitters will suffice.

GLASSWARE
Highball

ICE
Cubes to serve

GARNISH
Fresh cherry, orange twist

SERVES 1

45ml (1½fl oz) Talisker 57° North whisky
20ml (¾fl oz) Dolin red vermouth
4 dashes of Mazaniova liquorice bitters
Ginger ale, to top up

Bartender's Tip
Slow pour ginger ale to keep the bubbles large and vibrant.

Fill a highball glass with ice. Add all the ingredients except the ginger ale, then top up with more ice. Slowly pour in the ginger ale to just below the brim. Stir and garnish with a fresh cherry and an orange twist.

Calm Down, Deer

This cocktail is a take on the ubiquitous Old Fashioned. Aberlour A'Bunadh is another great non-chill-filtered, individual batch offering from Speyside. Matured in oloroso sherry casks, it's a wonderful pairing to the extremely sweet sherry reduction. Pedro Ximénez (PX) is an ultra dense, ultra sweet style of sherry made from the juice of sun-dried grapes. Barley coffee is a caffeine-free espresso alternative of Italian origin made from roasted barley. It is touted for its calming and soothing effects.

GLASSWARE
Rocks

ICE
Cubes to stir and to serve

GARNISH
None

First make the barley coffee PX reduction. Pour the PX sherry into a shallow saucepan over a medium heat. Reduce to about two-thirds of its original volume, then add the barley coffee and stir gently. Bottle in a sterilized container and refrigerate until ready to use.

To make the cocktail, half fill a chilled mixing glass with ice. Add all the ingredients and stir vigorously (A'Bunadh is 59.6% ABV and so will require extra dilution). Serve in a rocks glass and pair with rich chocolate truffles for a delicious after-dinner drink.

SERVES 1

50ml (1¾fl oz) Aberlour A'Bunadh whisky
10ml (2 tsp) barley coffee PX reduction (*see* below)
4 dashes of The Bitter Truth Old Time aromatic bitters

For the barley coffee PX reduction (Makes 60ml/2fl oz)
100ml (3½fl oz) PX sherry
1 tsp instant barley coffee powder

Bartender's Tip
Some craft whiskys have rather high ABVs so you may need to stir it more than you'd think necessary before serving, in order to melt down some of the ice and thin out the potent whisky.

Not For The Feint Hearted

This drink was designed with the famous bourbon boilermakers in mind. GlenDronach 15yo is one of my favourite Speyside expressions, with its full sherry nose and a hot, buttery, toffee palate with a sweet salt-caramel finish. Balanced with the bizarre juniper and malt notes of the Genever, concentrated herbaceous notes of the Chartreuse and citrus zing of the verbena, the ingredients are designed to enhance the go-to-hell big, juicy hops and fresh citrus notes of the London-based microbrewery's ale.

GLASSWARE
Beer tankard

ICE
Cubes to shake and to serve

GARNISH
Orange twist

SERVES 1

25ml (¾fl oz) GlenDronach 15yo Revival whisky
20ml (¾fl oz) Bokma Oude Genever gin
2 dashes of Chartreuse Elixir Vegetal liqueur
15ml (½fl oz) lemon verbena tincture
Beavertown Gamma Ray American Pale Ale, to top up

Bartender's Tip
I like to use local craft beers for my beer cocktails, as the depth of flavour is often vastly more interesting. However, they are often bottle-conditioned and can have a heavy deposit in the bottle that isn't to everyone's taste.

Add all the ingredients except the pale ale to a shaker with ice. Shake well, then double strain into a beer tankard (*see* page 219). Fill the tankard with ice, then slowly pour the pale ale to the brim. Garnish with an orange twist.

Eòrna agus Fiòn

This drink is designed to progress the age-old relationship between whisky and sherry casks. When war with France ended the practice of ageing whisky in French wine casks, casks from Jerez became the preferred choice. Rather than the more typical sweeter oloroso sherry casks used in malt whisky production, the Bruichladdich Sherry Classic uses the lighter fino, manzanilla and palo cortado sherry casks. I've tried to enhance this with the manzanilla sherry and to offset all that salty dryness with the pungent saffron and sweet Muscat grape reduction. Eòrna agus Fiòn means 'Barley and Wine' in Gaelic.

First make the saffron soda. Fill a soda siphon with water, add a pinch of saffron and charge with carbon dioxide. Refrigerate before serving – this will allow time for the saffron to infuse and for the liquid to chill.

To make the cocktail, fill a highball glass with ice. Add all the ingredients except the saffron soda. Stir gently, then top up with the saffron soda. Garnish with Muscat grapes.

GLASSWARE
Highball

ICE
Cubes to serve

GARNISH
Muscat grapes (or other grapes if Muscat are not in season)

SERVES 1

45ml (1½fl oz) Bruichladdich Sherry Classic whisky
15ml (½fl oz) manzanilla sherry
10ml (2 tsp) Muscat grape concentrate
130ml (4fl oz) saffron soda (*see* below)

For the saffron soda
Mineral or filtered water
1 pinch of saffron

You will also need
Soda siphon and carbon dioxide charges

Bartender's Tip
The trickiest part of this drink is the saffron soda. A tiny pinch will be enough to flavour a whole soda siphon. So, experiment with different measures before trying to impress your date with this drink.

Thee, Ferintosh! O Sadly Lost!

The somewhat esoteric name comes from a line from *Scotch Drink*, the Robert Burns poem written in 1785 about this wonderful spirit. It talks of the Ferintosh distillery in the northern Highlands, regarded as the first licensed distillery in Scotland from 1690 until the Wash Act withdrew the right to distil in 1784. As Ferintosh whisky is understandably hard to get a hold of, it seems appropriate instead to use one of Scotland's newest distilleries, the still-independent Arran distillery. It is situated on the Isle of Arran between the Scottish mainland and the Mull of Kintyre and is already garnering awards.

GLASSWARE
Hurricane

ICE
Cubes to shake, none to serve

GARNISH
Honeycomb, lemon twist

SERVES 1

50ml (1¾fl oz) Arran 10yo whisky
20ml (¾fl oz) Bergamot juice
20ml (¾fl oz) heather honey
2 dashes of Dr Adam Elmegirab's Teapot bitters
²⁄₃ egg white, preferably Burford Brown

Add all the ingredients to a shaker (without ice) and dry shake briefly, but vigorously (*see* page 219), then add ice and shake again (*see* method on page 105). Double strain through a tea strainer into a hurricane glass (*see* page 219) and garnish with a piece of honeycomb and a lemon twist.

Bartender's Tip
The vigorous shaking of the egg white is paramount in any sour recipe. If you really want to seal the deal, you can build the drink in a wide-mouth beaker and give it a blast with a stick blender.

The Provenance

This drink should come across as delicate and fresh, and is a tentative attempt to pair whisky with bubbles. With a mind to promote provenance, the Bruichladdich distillery uses only barley grown in Scotland (a rarity in recent years), and the ice cider and English sparkling wine are also both made from fruit grown from their own orchards/vineyards (also a rarity). Ice cider is a dessert drink made from late-harvested apples that are allowed to overripen and become naturally concentrated by the sub-zero temperatures of Québec – it needs more than eight times as many apples than a batch of dry cider.

GLASSWARE
Flute

ICE
Cubes to stir, none to serve

GARNISH
2 drops of light walnut oil, edible flower

SERVES 1

20ml (¾fl oz) Bruichladdich The Organic Scottish Barley whisky
20ml (¾fl oz) Canadian ice cider
110ml (4fl oz) Herbert Hall NV English sparkling wine, to top up

Add the whisky and the ice cider to a chilled mixing glass with ice. Stir until chilled. Add a splash of the sparkling wine to a chilled flute, then strain the cocktail into the glass. Top up with the remaining sparkling wine, add the walnut oil and garnish with an edible flower.

Bartender's Tip
With walnut oil, it's easy to get a darker, cheaper flavour. To avoid this, pick up any brand of organic walnut oil at your local health food store. The taste of this drink will justify the unusual ingredient!

BRANDY

'Brandy, *n.* A cordial
composed of one part
thunder-and-lightning,
one part remorse, two parts
bloody murder, one part
death-hell-and-the-grave
and four parts clarified Satan.
Dose, a headful all the time.
Brandy is said by Dr Johnson
to be the drink of heroes.
Only a hero will venture
to drink it.'
Ambrose Bierce,
The Devil's Dictionary

Recipes by Dino Koletsas

Reverend JW Simpson, UK

Brandy
by John Naughton

According to the 18th-century man of letters Dr Johnson, 'Claret is the liquor for boys, port for men; but he who aspires to be a hero must drink brandy.'

If that is indeed the case, then there must be a lot of people out there who are feeling very heroic at the moment, because currently brandy is booming. Either as a post-meal digestif or, increasingly commonly, as the basis for myriad varieties of cocktails, the drink that takes its name from the Dutch word *brandewijn* (meaning 'burnt wine'), and now finds itself routinely name-checked in hip-hop lyrics, has never been more popular.

Brandy, it should be noted, covers a multitude of beverages, ranging from the highly regarded such as Cognac to the happily discarded, lurking in the furthest recesses of the drinks cabinet. Think of any unwise holiday purchase of spirit – Metaxa, ouzo, grappa, for instance – and chances are you will find it classified as some kind of brandy.

Essentially, there are three different types of brandy, and it is not entirely unfair to think of them as the Good, the Bad and the Ugly. Grape brandy is very much the first type and comprises the aforementioned Cognac as well as Armagnac, the first distilled spirit in France. Portugal's Lourinhã and the more bracing Pisco from Peru (basis for the legendary Pisco Sour cocktail) still fall into this category. Next, we have fruit brandies, which include the likes of Calvados (made from French apples) through schnapps and slivovitz (plum brandy, essentially). Finally, there's pomace brandy, made from the seeds, skins and stems of grapes, which therefore exists in relation to Cognac in much the same way as the doner kebab does to filet mignon. Grappa and the fractionally less smooth grozdova and chacha are the usual suspects in this category.

Before noting the competing brands, it is as well to understand the different classifications that are standard to all brandies. All proper brandies have been aged to some degree, and the different letters attached to the drink simply identify how long that process has taken. As the classifications were decided by the French in relation to an English market, it is no surprise that there is a fair degree of disagreement about what each classification indicates, but it is generally accepted that AC indicates two years, while VS (Very Special or Superior), also known as Three Star, signifies a minimum of three years. The famous VSOP (Very Special/Superior Old Pale) denotes a five-year ageing process, XO (Extra Old) represents six years, while Hors d'Age ('beyond age') brandy is older than these categories – normally a minimum of ten years. A vintage brandy will carry a stamp indicating the year in which it was first stored.

All Cognacs are brandy, but not all brandies are Cognac. There is a strict set of criteria that define what constitutes the premier form of brandy. Firstly, it must be produced in the Charente or Charente-Maritime region of France, which lies just north of Bordeaux, and be made from at least 90 per cent Ugni Blanc grapes, with the remainder from certain other specified varieties.

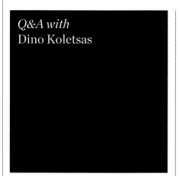

Q&A with
Dino Koletsas

How long have you been a bartender? Officially 15 years, but I've worked at my dad's restaurant on the Greek island of Zakynthos from the age of 10 every summer for 3 months.

What is your bartending philosophy? Simple, classically minded drinks are hard to beat, but you will never fully enjoy them if you are not in the right environment. That means the light, the music, the temperature of the venue and, of course, the company. I always strive to get those right to go with the drinks.

What is the key to making a great cocktail? Being able to see past your own likes and dislikes. This helps find the balance in any combination of ingredients – one can create cocktails that are great for others not just oneself.

What is your favourite cocktail ingredient at the moment? I'm really enjoying using herb-scented sherbets and shrubs. They have their own incredible way of adding a complex acidity to drinks.

Three great all-rounder brandies recommended by Dino Koletsas

1 Martell Cordon Bleu
2 Michel Couprie VSOP
3 Laird's 7$\frac{1}{2}$yo Applejack brandy

Fermentation will take up to three weeks, as no artificial sugars or chemicals may be added to speed up the process. When it is ready for distillation, this must be done first in copper pot stills before it is aged in barrels, which themselves must conform to strict guidelines (Tronçais or Limousin oak that has been dry-aged outdoors for between one and three years).

Given that the ageing process for Cognac can run into decades, it is no surprise that the drink carries with it a hefty price tag, a characteristic that has made it a natural constituent of hip-hop culture. Ever since Busta Rhymes, P Diddy and Pharrell released 'Pass the Courvoisier, Pt II' in 2002, Cognac – or yak, Remi, nyak, nak, Henn-dog or Henny, as it is also known – has been an essential status symbol, and sales have soared to the point where the US is now easily the main export market for the spirit. There's no denying the essential truth expressed in Snoop Dogg's 'Gz Up, Hoes Down', namely: 'Cognac is the drink that's drunk by Gs.'

The big four brands are Hennessy, Rémy Martin, Martell and Courvoisier. All have benefitted from Cognac's new-found fame, but each attempts its own marketing spin to ensure differentiation from the nak pack. Hennessy, for instance, has been leading the field in suggesting we try its wares blended with tea, entering into a partnership with upmarket French tea merchants, Théodor, to create Fine de Cognac & Tea. Embracing its upmarket reach, Hennessy also promotes Ellipse Cognac, which comes in an elliptical Baccarat crystal decanter, retailing at $6,500. No self-respecting gangsta (and is there any other kind?) should be without.

If Hennessy is aiming to carve out a niche in the upper reaches of the market, brands like Pierre Ferrand have enjoyed success by promoting themselves in connection with cocktails. Adventurous types might be drawn to the likes of the Twisted Rivoli, which mixes Cognac, apricot brandy and marmalade. However, updates on classics – such as the 75 D-Lux, which was invented at Bar Congress in Austin, Texas, and replaces the traditional gin of the French 75 with Cognac – have also proved popular.

Not that the classic brandy cocktails themselves are faring too badly. Notable among these is, of course, the Brandy Alexander, which mixes Cognac and crème de cacao to sweet effect and has always enjoyed an upmarket reputation, not least because it is supposed to have been named after a tsar. The Sidecar – Cognac, Grand Marnier and lemon juice – is similarly superior, with competing claims for its origin being The Ritz or Harry's Bar in Paris, or Buck's Club in London. No single individual has claimed responsibility for the Stinger, which though it can be made with other spirits is classically a mixture of Cognac and white crème de menthe. Perhaps its aftereffects were deemed too devastating for anyone to own up, but its popularity with American pilots in World War II suggests its origins lie on the other side of the Atlantic.

Doubtless, those flyboys, who knew a thing or two about heroism, had just taken the words of Dr Johnson to heart.

Cyzerac

Although strictly a type of mead (created by the fermentation of honey with apple juice), the Cyser has inspired the naming of this twist on a Sazerac. This cocktail champions the Britishness of its two core ingredients: mead and apple brandy. Absinthe is a wonderful partner to both the honey and the apple flavours, while the two types of bitters add depth of flavour, complexity and a longer finish to the drink. The lemon zest adds a crisp, clean aroma when sipping.

GLASSWARE
Rocks

ICE
Crushed and cubes to stir, one large cube to serve

GARNISH
Lemon twist

SERVES 1

15ml (½fl oz) Pernod absinthe
20ml (¾fl oz) Lindisfarne mead
50ml (1¾fl oz) Somerset Cider Brandy 5yo
7ml (1½ tsp) apple syrup (*see* Bartender's Tip)
2 dashes of Peychaud's bitters
2 dashes of Bob's Abbott's bitters

Add crushed ice and the absinthe to a chilled rocks glass and leave to chill. Add the remaining ingredients to a mixing glass with ice and stir until well chilled. Pour the absinthe and ice out of the rocks glass and discard. Strain the now well-chilled cocktail into the absinthe-rinsed glass containing a large ice cube. Zest the lemon twist to release the oils over the surface of the drink (*see* page 219), then use to garnish the cocktail.

Bartender's Tip
To make the apple syrup: gently heat fresh apple juice (not from concentrate) with an equal volume of caster sugar until the sugar has dissolved – do not let it boil.

Sangria Grande

The Sangria Grande is a bolder expression of the classic summer drink from Spain and Portugal, and draws more on the quality of the brandy. Spanish brandy is a very different creature to its French cousin – it is primarily made in Catalonia and in Jerez and works very well in this cocktail (but a French brandy will work as well). And don't forget, this recipe can be scaled-up easily to be served in a punch bowl for sharing.

GLASSWARE
Highball

ICE
Cubes to shake and to serve

GARNISH
Seasonal fruit and herbs

SERVES 1

30ml (1fl oz) Gran Duque D'Alba Brandy de Jerez
40ml (1¼fl oz) red wine (a young Rioja will work well)
20ml (¾fl oz) orange juice
5ml (1 tsp) cherry liqueur
2 dashes of Bob's Abbott's bitters
10g (½oz) Seville orange and thyme sherbet (*see* below)

For the Seville orange and thyme sherbet
(Makes 400g/13oz)
6 Seville oranges
100g (3½oz) caster sugar
6 thyme leaves

Bartender's Tip
Brandy de Jerez is often made by sherry producers who use old sherry casks and the solera method to age their brandy, which gives it a sweeter character and a richer colour.

First make the sherbet. Grate the peel of the oranges into a bowl, then press the sugar into the peel until it has mixed well and you have a coarse paste. Add the thyme leaves and crush into the paste. Juice the oranges (you want about 400ml/14fl oz of juice), then mix the juice into the paste until the sugar has dissolved. Leave the mixture to blend for a few hours, stirring occasionally, then strain the mixture as finely as you can. The sherbet will keep well in a refrigerator for up to a week.

To make the Sangria Grande, add all the ingredients to a shaker with ice and shake vigorously until thoroughly chilled. Strain into a chilled highball glass over ice. Garnish with any fruits and herbs that are in season.

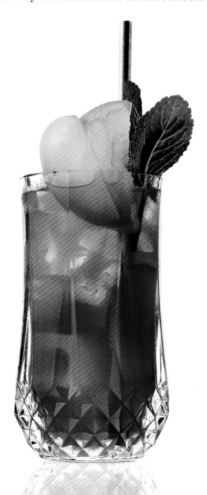

Vieux Carré

Originally created in the Thirties by Walter Bergeron in the previous incarnation of the Carousel bar at the Monteleone Hotel, the Vieux Carré has its soul in New Orleans's Old Quarter from where it hails and after which it is named. The drink reflects the diverse culture of its hometown. A complex yet ultra-smooth drinking cocktail, it should be noted that a good-quality VSOP Cognac (such as Michel Couprie VSOP with its grapey richness) or Rémy Martin Cœur de Cognac (with its light floral notes) deliver very different outcomes to this drink.

GLASSWARE
Rocks

ICE
Cubes to stir and to serve

GARNISH
Lemon twist, maraschino cherry

SERVES 1

20ml (¾fl oz) French brandy (Cognac or Armagnac)
20ml (¾fl oz) Four Roses Yellow Label bourbon
20ml (¾fl oz) Byrrh Grand Quinquina
8ml (1½ tsp) Benedictine
2 dashes of Bitter Truth Creole bitters
1 dash of Angostura bitters

Bartender's Tip
Adding vermouth has a great impact on this drink – I'd recommend trying something like Sacred Spiced vermouth or even a dry (French) style of vermouth if you fancy.

Add all the ingredients to a mixing glass with ice. Stir until well chilled, mixed and diluted to your taste. Strain into a rocks glass over ice. Zest the lemon twist to release the oils over the surface of the drink (*see* page 219), then use to garnish the cocktail along with a maraschino cherry.

Applejack Rabbit à la Simpson

This drink first appeared in *Here's How!* by Judge Jr in 1927. It features as its base the USA's gift to the world of brandy (by way of a Scottish immigrant called William Laird): Applejack, an apple-based spirit once known as Jersey Lightning. Today, applejack brandy is making a resurgence following a long time in obscurity and is now giving Calvados – its famous French cousin – a run for its money in the cocktail stakes. I also like to use the bitter, sour Seville orange when in season as it adds an extra dimension to this drink – though be warned: you may have to reduce the lemon juice.

GLASSWARE
Rocks

ICE
Cubes to shake and to serve

GARNISH
Grated cinnamon, cinnamon stick, orange slice

SERVES 1

50ml (1¾fl oz) Laird's Applejack infused with cinnamon
20ml (¾fl oz) lemon juice
25ml (¾fl oz) orange juice
10–15ml (2–3 tsp) maple syrup

Add all the ingredients to a shaker with ice, then shake vigorously until the shaker is frosted on the outside and almost too cold to handle. Strain into a chilled rocks glass over ice. Garnish with grated cinnamon, an orange slice and a cinnamon stick.

Bartender's Tip
Maple syrup is classified in grades both in the USA and Canada, where the majority of the world's supply comes from. The quality that you prefer (lighter or heavier) will affect how much should be added to your drink.

Double Stinger

Dating back at least as far as 1917, the stinger was traditionally an after-dinner drink, combining the richness of brandy and the digestive properties of crème de menthe. The fresh mint adds a lighter dimension to the drink that can actually be enjoyed at any time, which is also why I really like the drier, punchier style the Armagnac brings to this drink. To borrow a phrase from Cary Grant in the 1957 movie *Kiss Them For Me*: 'Stingers, and keep them coming.'

GLASSWARE
Sherry

ICE
Cubes to shake, none to serve

GARNISH
Mint sprig, lemon twist (discarded)

SERVES 1

40ml (1¼fl oz) Château de Laubade VSOP Bas-Armagnac
15ml (½fl oz) white crème de menthe
8 mint leaves

Add all the ingredients to a shaker with ice, then shake vigorously. Double strain into a sherry glass (*see* page 219). Zest the lemon twist to release the oils over the surface of the drink (*see* page 219). Discard the twist, then garnish with a mint sprig.

Bartender's Tip
By swapping vodka for brandy, you will make a White Stinger. Sticking with brandy, but using green crème de menthe instead of white, will give you a Green Hornet.

Coffee Cocktail

This drink first appears in the 1887 version of 'Professor' Jerry Thomas's *How to Mix Drinks*, and yet, despite its name, this drink contains no coffee. Nor for that matter, the defining ingredient that would make it a cocktail of its time: bitters. I have chosen to steer away from the classic balance, which calls for port as the primary alcoholic ingredient. To compensate, I also use a sweeter Spanish brandy in equal measure to the port. The sugar syrup adds to the body of the drink, and the egg shaken in the drink provides the rich texture and silky mouthfeel as well as the coffee-like appearance.

GLASSWARE
Martini

ICE
Cubes to shake, none to serve

GARNISH
Grated nutmeg

SERVES 1

35ml (1fl oz) Romate Brandy de Jerez
35ml (1fl oz) tawny port
10ml (2 tsp) sugar syrup
1 small egg

Add all the ingredients to a shaker (without ice) and dry shake briefly, but vigorously (*see* page 219). Add ice and shake again until the outside is frosted. Strain into a chilled Martini glass and garnish with grated nutmeg.

Bartender's Tip
To try the original Coffee Cocktail, use two shots of port to one shot of brandy.

East India Cocktail

The East India Cocktail is another 19th-century classic. Initially listed in *Harry Johnson's Bartenders' Manual* in 1882, this drink has a surprising dryness to it despite the absence of any natural sour ingredient to balance the multiple sweet elements. A curious outcome, but all the more pleasing for it. I list the easily obtainable Angostura bitters for this drink as the original Boker's no longer exists (a modern version of those bitters is now back on the market, but I cannot vouch for its historical accuracy!). And I have recommended a higher strength Cognac as I enjoy the added kick.

GLASSWARE
Sherry or Martini

ICE
Cubes to shake, none to serve

GARNISH
Lemon twist, maraschino cherry

SERVES 1

40ml (1¼fl oz) Louis Royer Force 53 Cognac
5ml (1 tsp) pineapple syrup
10ml (2 tsp) maraschino liqueur
5ml (1 tsp) orange curaçao
1 dash of Angostura bitters

Add all the ingredients to a shaker with ice and shake vigorously until thoroughly chilled. Strain into a chilled sherry or Martini glass. Garnish with a lemon twist and a maraschino cherry.

Bartender's Tip
Some later versions of the East India Cocktail call for raspberry syrup instead of pineapple – this is worth a try for a very different and much fruitier drink.

Little Bird Pickford

The original cocktail that inspired this drink was made in Cuba in the Twenties and named in honour of 'America's Sweetheart', the silent film star Mary Pickford. The Peruvian brandy featured here is clean and fruity and adds a distinctive rock-candy flavour to this drink. The name is part inspired by Miss Pickford's nickname 'Little Mary' and the translation of the Quechua word *pisco* which is 'little bird'.

GLASSWARE
Sherry or Martini

ICE
Cubes to shake, none to serve

GARNISH
Lime twist (discarded),
maraschino cherry,
pineapple wedge

SERVES 1

50ml (1¾fl oz) 1615 Pisco
5ml (1 tsp) maraschino liqueur
15ml (½fl oz) pineapple juice
15ml (½fl oz) pomegranate
 syrup
1 lime wedge

Add all the ingredients except the lime wedge into shaker with ice. Squeeze in the juice from the lime wedge and drop the wedge in the shaker too, then shake vigorously until chilled and diluted. Strain into a chilled sherry or Martini glass. Zest the lime twist to release the oils over the surface of the drink (*see* page 219). Discard the twist, drop a maraschino cherry into the glass and garnish with a pineapple wedge.

Bartender's Tip
The original Mary Pickford cocktail recipe calls for a light rum. I have replaced it with Peruvian Pisco, but feel free to try it as originally intended.

Brandtea Punch

This drink draws greatly on the Victorian enthusiasm for punch. Fresh and clean to drink, Brandtea Punch is best prepared in advance to allow the ingredients to mellow together in a refrigerator and then served in a grand punch bowl for everyone to partake of around a table.

GLASSWARE
Half-pint beer mug

ICE
Large cubes

GARNISH
Orange slice, lemon slice, mint sprig, grated nutmeg

SERVES 1

50ml (1¾fl oz) Courvoisier VSOP Cognac
60ml (2fl oz) strong Earl Grey tea (*see* Bartender's Tip)
20ml (¾fl oz) lemon sherbet (*see* page 14)
2 dashes of Angostura bitters
7ml (1½ tsp) maraschino liqueur
10ml (2 tsp) lemon juice

Add all the ingredients to a half-pint beer mug, then add some large ice cubes. Stir briefly to mix and chill, then top up with more ice if required. Garnish with orange and lemon slices, a fresh sprig of mint and a little grated nutmeg.

Bartender's Tip
To make the Earl Grey tea: steep 1 teaspoon of good-quality loose-leaf Earl Grey tea per 150ml (¼ pint) of freshly boiled water. Strain when you have a strong tea, but do not allow to stew. Cool before use.

Raisin' 'n' Blazin'

This hot cocktail is almost as much about the showmanship of the creation as it is about the flavour of the drink. Almost. The key is to pour the flaming concoction two or three times between heatproof tankards – that way you do not burn off all the alcohol. For this cocktail, use Metaxa, a proprietary Greek brandy blended with the famous Muscat wines of Lemnos. Metaxa uses its own star-rating system based on the old Cognac rating system – the more stars the longer the ageing and the drier the end product.

GLASSWARE
Brandy balloon

ICE
None

GARNISH
Orange slice, lemon slice, clove-studded pineapple slice

SERVES 1

70ml (2¼fl oz) Metaxa 7 Stars
50g (2oz) pistachios
100g (3½oz) raisins
7ml (1½ tsp) passion fruit syrup
2 dashes of Angostura bitters
2 dashes of Bob's Abbott's bitters
30ml (1fl oz) water

You will also need
2 heatproof tankards
1 carafe filled with room-temperature water
1 wet tea towel to hand, just in case you need to put out a stray flame!

Bartender's Tip
This is a theatrical cocktail and caution is recommended. When you get as far as serving the drink, always ensure the glass hasn't become too hot to sip from.

First infuse the Metaxa. Pour the Metaxa into a sterilized jar and add the pistachios and raisins. Leave to infuse for a minimum of 2 days at room temperature.

To make the cocktail, strain the Metaxa into one of the heatproof tankards (the discarded raisins make a yummy boozy nibble).

Warm the infused Metaxa, passion fruit syrup and bitters in the heatproof tankard – this makes it easier to light – but be sure not to let it boil. When the spirit is warm, light it in the first tankard. Steadily pour it into the second tankard ensuring the flame doesn't extinguish. (Practise and caution will allow you to build up the distance between the two tankards during the pour, which makes for an impressive party trick.) Repeat the pour 2–3 times and then pour into the brandy balloon – by this point the cocktail will be hot. Drop the pieces of fruit garnish into the balloon, then pour in the water. This should extinguish the last of the flames, should any linger, and it will also help bring the temperature of the cocktail back down to drinkable and temper the volatile alcoholic fumes.

Pineapple-Fir Julep

This cocktail is inspired by the earliest incarnations of the julep as an alcoholic libation dating back to the early 1800s. For this variation, Armagnac is used as the main spirit as the raw style holds up better in a longer drink. The Douglas fir liqueur brings an incredible citrus and pine character to the drink and a Christmassy aroma to proceedings, while the orange peel cuts through the sweetness. Peach bitters add depth and the mint gives this drink its classic freshness.

GLASSWARE
Rocks or julep tin

ICE
Crushed to stir and to serve

GARNISH
Douglas fir tincture (*see* method), orange slice, mint sprig

SERVES 1

15ml (½fl oz) Douglas fir liqueur (*see* below)
40ml (1¼fl oz) Château de Laubade VSOP Bas-Armagnac
2 thin slices of pineapple quarters
8 mint leaves
2 pieces of orange peel
1 dash of peach bitters

For the Douglas fir liqueur (Makes 1 litre/1¾ pints)
100g (3½oz) small Douglas fir branches
1 litre bottle (1¾ pints) vodka (high-proof 50% ABV)
400g (13oz) caster sugar

Bartender's Tip
If you don't fancy making your own, the Clear Creek Distillery in the US produce a Douglas Fir Eau de Vie that you can order online.

First make the Douglas fir liqueur. Steep pieces of branch in the vodka using 100g (3½oz) of branch for every 1 litre (1¾ pints) of spirit. Leave for a day or two depending on the time of year. Strain and set aside 100ml (3½fl oz) of the tincture for a garnish. To the remainder, add the sugar and stir until it has fully dissolved.

To make the drink, add all the cocktail ingredients to the bottom of a julep tin and press the mint leaves and orange peels gently to extract the oils. Add crushed ice until the tin is two-thirds full, then stir until chilled. Top up with more crushed ice and garnish with a mint sprig and an orange slice. Spray a little bit of the Douglas fir tincture that was set aside earlier from an atomizer over the drink.

Meadow Queen

This drink is directly inspired by one of the all-time classic cocktails, the Brandy Crusta (so named because of the crust of sugar on the rim). Yet another drink that derives from New Orleans in the mid-19th century, the original Crusta was created by Joseph Santina who kept bar at the Jewel of the South in Gravier Street. In this variation, maraschino liqueur is replaced with the wild European herb meadowsweet to evoke an aroma of the British countryside. It is a smell so familiar yet almost impossible to pinpoint for a city dweller.

GLASSWARE
Sherry or Martini

ICE
Cubes to shake, none to serve

GARNISH
Meadowsweet sugar
(*see* method), lemon wedge,
maraschino cherry, long
orange twist

SERVES 1

40ml (1¼fl oz) Rémy Martin
   VSOP Cognac
10ml (2 tsp) triple sec
20ml (¾fl oz) lemon juice
15ml (½fl oz) meadowsweet
   liqueur (*see* below)
1 dash of Angostura bitters

**For the meadowsweet liqueur
(Makes 1 litre/1¾ pints)**
30g (1oz) dried meadowsweet
1 litre (1¾ pints) high-proof
   neutral spirit (eg 50% ABV vodka)
450g (14½oz) caster sugar

For the meadowsweet sugar
100g (3½oz) brown sugar
10g (½oz) dried meadowsweet

Bartender's Tip
For an extra special serve,
prepare the sugar rim in
advance and leave it to
harden, thereby forming
a hard crust. Joe Santina
would surely approve.

Make the meadowsweet liqueur in advance. Steep the dried meadowsweet in the high-proof neutral spirit for 2 days. Strain, add the sugar to the liquid and stir until it has fully dissolved.

To make the meadowsweet sugar, place the brown sugar and dried meadowsweet in a blender, then blitz to a fine powder. Keep in a dry, airtight jar.

To make the cocktail, add all the ingredients to a shaker with plenty of ice and shake vigorously until well chilled. Coat the rim of a sherry or Martini glass in some lemon juice squeezed from a wedge, then dip it into the meadowsweet sugar ensuring it is evenly coated; wipe off the excess from inside and out with the lemon wedge. Strain the cocktail into the glass and drop in a maraschino cherry. Zest the orange twist to release the oils over the surface of the drink (*see* page 219), then rest it around the inner rim of the glass.

Japanese Jack Rose

The Jack Rose was popular in the Twenties and Thirties, but its origin remains open to debate. The most popular theory links the cocktail to a small-time New York gangster and gambler called 'Bald' Jack Rose who favoured a decent slug of applejack brandy with lemon and grenadine. This twist keeps the applejack, but adds the complexity of a rose tincture – taking advantage of roses' botanical relationship with apples (they are in the same family). The rose adds another layer to the drink, especially when adding the aromatic spray to finish it off.

GLASSWARE
Martini or wine

ICE
Cubes to shake, none to serve

GARNISH
Candied rose petal, Japanese Rose Tincture (*see* Bartender's Tip)

SERVES 1

50ml (1¾fl oz) Laird's Applejack
20ml (¾fl oz) lime juice
10ml (2 tsp) Japanese rose tincture (*see* Bartender's Tip)
15ml (½fl oz) pomegranate syrup

Add all the ingredients to a shaker with ice and shake until well chilled. Strain into a chilled Martini or wine glass and spray some rose tincture from an atomizer over the drink. Garnish with a candied rose petal (if using).

Bartender's Tip
For the Japanese rose tincture: steep 10g (½oz) of edible rose petals in 100ml (3½fl oz) of high-proof neutral spirit, (eg 50% ABV vodka), until the colour leaches from the petals. Do not allow to stew. Strain, then chill.

The Vicar's Fix

This particular Fix creates a tasty and unusual flavour combination. The Cognac merges deliciously (if surprisingly) together with the 'boiled sweet' flavour of the banana liqueur and the earthy flavours of the herb syrup. To finish the drink off, lime juice provides a souring balance while the bitters lend a depth and subtle spice. This cocktail probably shouldn't work...but it really does!

GLASSWARE
Sherry or Martini

ICE
Cubes to shake, none to serve

GARNISH
Lime twist, rosemary sprig (optional)

SERVES 1

40ml (1¼fl oz) Hennessy Fine de Cognac
10ml (2 tsp) crème de banane
10ml (2 tsp) herb syrup (*see* below)
20ml (¾fl oz) lime juice
10ml (2 tsp) apple juice
1 egg white (optional)
1 dash of Peychaud's bitters

For the herb syrup
(Makes 150ml/¼ pint)
1 sprig of thyme
1 sprig of rosemary
1 sprig of oregano
1 sprig of lavender
100g (3½oz) caster sugar
100ml (3½fl oz) filtered water

Bartender's Tip
By adding the egg white to this cocktail, you can add a little more texture to the drink. For a cleaner, crisper concoction, leave it out.

First make the syrup. Put all the syrup ingredients in a large saucepan and heat until the sugar has dissolved. Remove from the heat and leave to infuse and cool. Strain, then bottle in a sterilized container and refrigerate until ready to use.

To make the cocktail, add all the ingredients except the bitters to a shaker with ice and shake until thoroughly chilled. Strain into a sherry or Martini glass and add a dash of bitters on top. Garnish with a lime twist and a sprig of rosemary if liked.

CHAMPAGNE

'Too much of anything is bad, but too much champagne is just right.'
F. Scott Fitzgerald

Recipes by Agostino Perrone

The Connaught Bar, London

Champagne
by Dominic Bliss

£1.2 million. That's the price for a single bottle of Gout de Diamants, the world's most expensive champagne. Admittedly, the lion's share of that figure is thanks to the solid gold bottle label bejewelled with a single 19-carat diamond, yet the sparkling liquid inside is no doubt fairly special.

No other drink yet invented by man commands such awe, such reverence as champagne. Legend has it that it was invented at the end of the 17th century by a monk called Dom Pérignon, who famously declared on his first sip, 'Brothers, I am drinking the stars!' However, the facts are probably more prosaic, as there is evidence that it was invented in the 1660s by an English scientist, Christopher Merret. At any rate, the drink's mythical status as king of all wines has grown with every passing century. The bubbles still show no sign of bursting.

Much of this myth is down to canny marketing and product placement. But the debauched French royals of the pre-Revolutionary 18th century had a fair bit to do with it, too. Philippe II, Duke of Orléans, who was Regent of France for Louis XV in the early part of the century, apparently spent most of his time either seducing mistresses or getting drunk on champagne...probably both. Relations between champagne producers and the royal family grew very friendly indeed, so that Paris's fashionable upper classes soon began emulating their rulers in guzzling beaucoup de bubbly. In 1728, Louis XV signed a royal decree allowing champagne wines (but no other types) to be transported in bottles rather than the traditional barrels. Suddenly, using English-invented cork stoppers and stronger glass bottles, the champagne producers of the day were able to ship bottled bubbles to rich customers all over Europe.

But it was not until Europe's rapidly growing bourgeoisie started developing a taste for the wine (and a disposable income) that mass production was called for. As Becky Sue Epstein writes in her book *Champagne: A Global History*, 'Champagne became the first table wine to be shipped all over the world. [It] was an aspiration for the nouveaux riches, merchants and other moderately wealthy people who were not aristocratic by birth. It was the symbol of glamour.'

The mystique of champagne has a lot to do with the strict rules of the Comité Champagne that now govern its manufacture. These include the exclusive use of Chardonnay, Pinot Noir and Pinot Meunier grapes (and occasionally other varieties), which must be grown on the 34,000 hectares (84,000 acres) of officially sanctioned vineyards in the Champagne region. The grapes must be pruned, harvested by hand, pressed, stored and aged (for a minimum of 15 months) in a specific way. Unlike most still wines, champagne undergoes a secondary fermentation during which carbonation occurs.

There are currently more than 5,000 champagne producers in all, ranging from tiny artisans up to the major *Maisons de Champagne* such as Bollinger, Piper-Heidsieck, Krug, Lanson, Laurent-Perrier, Moët & Chandon, Mumm and Veuve Clicquot. All are understandably highly protective of their product.

Q&A with
Agostino Perrone

Almost as much ink as grape juice has been spilled in legal efforts over the last 130 years to ensure that no other sparkling wine hijacks the precious champagne name. And the protectionism works. In 2013, according to the Comité Champagne, 304 million bottles of champagne were shipped out, with a value of €4.3 billion.

Of course, not all genuine champagne is worthy of its name. As wine writer Hugh Johnson says, 'There are champagnes and champagnes.' In recent years many experts have rated certain Australian and English sparkling wines above their champagne counterparts. The medium-priced champagnes you can pick up at some stores often pale in comparison to cheaper cavas, proseccos and crémants.

Products with near-mythical status will always have an unfair advantage over their rivals. Blame an organization that has existed since 1882 (just after French vineyards were decimated by phylloxera), now called the Union des Maisons de Champagne (UMC). Later threatened by other sparkling-wine producers elsewhere in the world, the UMC has vigorously marketed its product as the ultimate symbol of luxury ever since.

The quirky ceremonies associated with champagne have also helped build its reputation. It is almost always served in a flute glass, whose narrow shape ensures the bubbles don't dissipate too quickly. Occasionally you will receive it in a coupe glass. According to legend, this was modelled on the left breast of Marie Antoinette, as a birthday gift to her husband, Louis XVI of France. Seasoned sommeliers will pour champagne one-handed, with a thumb in the deep base of the bottle, and into a tilted glass to avoid a frothy head of bubbles.

There are apparently 47 million or so bubbles in a standard bottle of champagne, and 90psi of pressure – enough energy to give a projected cork a top speed of 100mph (160kph). The mushroom-shaped corks and the wire muselets used to secure them, combined with the elegant, feminine shape of the bottle, add to the sense of ceremony. In sport, winners are expected to shake up their trophy bottle of champagne before popping the cork and spraying fans and fellow sportsmen. In boating circles it is churlish to launch even the most humble seafaring vessel without smashing a bottle of champers against her hull.

But the most showy ceremony of all must be what is known as *sabrage*. Dating back to the Napoleonic Wars, this involves decapitating the entire neck and head of the bottle, cork and all, with a sabre. Over the years it has seen the demise of many a careless waiter's thumb. Nevertheless, it is sure to inject even the poorest-quality champagne with a wonderful taste.

As long as swordsmen continue to inflict *sabrage*, champagne's position as king of wines is secure. In 2013, an American, Mitch Ancona, won a place in *Guinness World Records* by sabering 34 champagne bottles in the space of a minute. No thumbs were harmed in the process.

Mount Street Cobbler

A Cobbler is traditionally a rich blend of a spirit or liqueur with wine or fortified wine and fruit, all served in a goblet glass over cracked ice 'cobbles'. Pineapple forms the main body of the Mount Street Cobbler and the vermouth adds an elegant spiciness with hints of vanilla and citrus. The maraschino liqueur gives the drink a dry length, while the champagne adds sparkle and vitality.

GLASSWARE
Wine

ICE
Cubes to stir, none to serve

GARNISH
3 dried pineapple slivers, maraschino cherry, grated nutmeg

SERVES 1

20ml (¾fl oz) pineapple purée
15ml (½fl oz) Martini Bianco vermouth
10ml (2 tsp) lemon juice
10ml (2 tsp) maraschino liqueur
50ml (1¾fl oz) NV Blanc de Blancs champagne

Add all the ingredients to a mixing glass with ice. Stir gently, then strain into a chilled wine glass. Garnish with slivers of dried pineapple, a maraschino cherry and grated nutmeg to taste.

Bartender's Tip
Make sure you taste your cocktail before serving. Fresh ingredients tend to change according to the time of the year and the supplier. Please use your nose and palate to ensure the flavours are balanced.

Peach Cardamom Bellini

Originally created by legendary bartender Giuseppe Cipriani at Harry's Bar, Venice, in the Thirties, the Bellini was named after the 15th-century Venetian painter Giovanni Bellini in 1948. He had a penchant for using rich pinks on his canvases, which echo the drink's pink hue. It's an Italian classic that should be the cornerstone of every home cocktail party as it's so easy to make. I've added cardamom to the original recipe to highlight the freshness of the drink and bring some spicy notes to the palate, while the Galliano adds real depth and silkiness.

GLASSWARE
Flute

ICE
Cubes to stir, none to serve

GARNISH
None

SERVES 1

25ml (¾fl oz) peach purée
10ml (2 tsp) Galliano L'Autentico liqueur
120ml (4fl oz) prosecco
5 drops of green cardamom essence

Bartender's Tip
This is true of all cocktails, but especially with fruit-based beauties: always use fresh juice and purée. For this, make sure your peaches are ripe, and it helps if they are fridge-cold.

Add all the ingredients to a mixing glass with ice. Stir gently, then strain into a chilled champagne flute.

Fleurissimo

This is considered one of my most refined signature cocktails. I originally designed it to honour Grace Kelly, who always stayed at the Connaught. It's actually named after her favourite fragrance, which was commissioned for her wedding to Prince Rainier of Monaco. The Cognac's big personality is smoothed by the violet liqueur, which also enhances the brandy's floral notes. The sugar cube infused with the bitters dissolves slowly so the taste develops minute by minute. Finally, the champagne marries the crisp notes of the cocktail together.

Place the sugar cube in a chilled champagne coupe, add the Cognac and the violet liqueur, then top up with the champagne. Garnish with the rose petals and a couple of sugar diamonds.

GLASSWARE
Coupe

ICE
None

GARNISH
2 rose petals, 2 sugar diamonds

SERVES 1

1 sugar cube infused with Peychaud's bitters
15ml (¾fl oz) Rémy Martin VSOP Cognac
5ml (1 tsp) violet liqueur
120ml (4fl oz) NV champagne

Bartender's Tip
Infusing the sugar cube with bitters is simple: just add a couple of dashes over each cube and leave them to soak in.

Old Cuban

Audrey Saunders created this drink in 2004 at the legendary Pegu Club in New York and it's already become a modern classic. Rum, mint and lime are a classic combination of Caribbean ingredients, but Audrey elevated them to another level by enriching the fruity and crisp notes with the champagne.

GLASSWARE
Martini

ICE
Cubes to shake, none to serve

GARNISH
Sugar-coated mint sprig

Add all the ingredients except the champagne to a shaker with ice. Shake well, then double strain (*see* page 219) into a chilled Martini glass and top up with the champagne. Garnish with a mint sprig dipped in caster sugar.

SERVES 1

35ml (1fl oz) Diplomático Blanco Reserva rum
15ml (½fl oz) lime juice
10ml (2 tsp) sugar syrup
8 mint leaves
75ml (2½fl oz) NV champagne

Bartender's Tip
For the full Audrey Saunders experience, garnish with a sugar-coated vanilla pod: take split vanilla pods, cut into 5cm (2in) sticks and store them in a jar of sugar for a week or so, after which you can use as required.

Italian Spritz Punch

I've used this recipe to link Italian cocktail culture (it uses two of the most iconic Italian spirits) with the fascinating history of British drinking culture, so I've served it in a punch bowl. I love the idea of sharing a drink in the same way you would share a meal. It's the perfect thing to serve at a celebration or special event. A classic Spritz mixes Aperol and champagne (or prosecco). Here, I've added Galliano to bring out the bouquet of floral, spicy notes of the other ingredients, lending it a subtle complexity. The citrus element gives fragrance and makes the combination even more refreshing.

GLASSWARE
Punch bowl and punch cups

ICE
3–4 large chunks

GARNISH
Cucumber slices, orange slices, lemon slices

SERVES 6

90ml (3fl oz) Galliano
L'Autentico liqueur
90ml (3fl oz) Aperol
750ml (1¼ pints) NV champagne

Bartender's Tip
Use large chunks of ice rather than cubes. These will melt more slowly and will soften the drink gradually rather than dilute it quickly.

Pour all the ingredients into a punch bowl, add 3–4 large chunks of ice and mix well. Garnish with the cucumber and orange and lemon slices.

William's Punch

Created by my dear friend, colleague and cocktail companion, Rusty Cerven, senior mixologist at the Connaught Bar, this recipe won the Bols Around The World Competition in 2013. Named after King William III (William of Orange), who helped popularize genever (also known as Dutch gin) in England, it's a quintessentially British blend using both rhubarb and lemon sherbet.

GLASSWARE
Wine

ICE
Cubes to stir and to serve

GARNISH
Grated nutmeg, lemon twist

SERVES 1

35ml (1fl oz) Bols Genever
20ml (¾fl oz) rhubarb juice
20ml (¾fl oz) lemon sherbet
  (*see* page 14)
10ml (2 tsp) violet liqueur
NV champagne, to top up

Add all the ingredients except for the champagne into a mixing glass with ice. Stir gently then strain into a red wine glass with ice and top up with the champagne. Garnish with a lemon twist and grated nutmeg to taste.

Bartender's Tip
Take the time to track down a bottle of genever. As mixable as a white spirit but with the complexity and sophistication of a brown spirit, genever is unique.

Japanese Affair

This long drink is mellow and full-bodied, yet refreshing at the same time. The fruity, spicy, roasted notes of the Japanese whisky sit alongside the zesty aromatic freshness of the yuzu, while the green tea is subtle, dry and delicate. The vintage champagne is the final flourish, adding a hint of sparkling citrus.

GLASSWARE
Wine

ICE
Frozen lava stones to serve

GARNISH
Butterflied sliver of dried pineapple, maraschino cherry

SERVES 1

¼ **tsp** Japanese matcha (powdered green tea)
10ml **(2 tsp)** sugar syrup
30ml **(1fl oz)** Hibiki 17yo whisky
15ml **(½fl oz)** yuzu juice
120ml **(4fl oz)** vintage Blanc de Blancs champagne

Bartender's Tip
Yuzu is an East Asian citrus, a kind of cross between a mandarin and grapefruit. It has a distinct aromatic aroma and intense citrusy flavour and is becoming increasingly available in the West.

Blend the matcha with the sugar syrup to make a green tea syrup. Pour into a shaker and add all the remaining ingredients, except the champagne. Dry shake (*see* page 219), then strain into a delicate wine glass containing a few frozen lava stones. Top up with the champagne and garnish with a butterflied sliver of dried pineapple and a maraschino cherry.

Pink Royale

This is a sophisticated upgrade of the very popular Kir Royale. The pink peppercorns add a sensational fresh spiciness, while the vermouth gives depth and complexity and matches with the fruity notes of the crème de cassis. Absinthe adds a dash of freshness that cuts through the viscosity of the drink, and the champagne brings all the elements together.

GLASSWARE
Flute

ICE
None

GARNISH
None

SERVES 1

10ml (2 tsp) pink peppercorn infusion (*see below*)
10ml (2 tsp) Martini Gran Lusso vermouth
2 dashes of French-style absinthe
120ml (4fl oz) NV Blanc de Blancs champagne

For the pink peppercorn infusion (Makes 100ml/3½fl oz)
15g (½oz) pink peppercorns, lightly crushed
100ml (3½fl oz) crème de cassis

You will also need
Cream whipper and **2** nitrous oxide charges

Bartender's Tip
Don't panic! Pink peppercorns are not part of the peppercorn family. They are actually milder in flavour, have a soft texture and share taste notes with juniper berries and aniseed.

First make the infusion. Mix the pink peppercorns with the crème de cassis. Pour the mixture into a cream siphon, use 2 charges and let the mixture rest for 1 hour. Carefully open the top to release the air, then strain the infused mix and bottle in a sterilized container until ready to use.

To make the cocktail, add all the ingredients except the champagne to a chilled flute and top up with chilled champagne.

Soyer au Champagne

Dating back to the Forties (or the late 1800s, if you believe some rumours), the Soyer au Champagne (Silk with Champagne) became a staple at high-class cocktail parties. Although champagne and ice cream may sound like a strange combination, it's the perfect mix of dessert and cocktail. The complexity and fruitiness of the ingredients complements the vanilla ice cream, while the champagne adds a final fizz of excitement. It was said to be a favourite of Queen Victoria, so consider it a cocktail fit for a queen...

GLASSWARE
Coupe

ICE
Cubes to stir, none to serve

GARNISH
None

SERVES 1

10ml (2 tsp) maraschino liqueur
10ml (2 tsp) pineapple juice
10ml (2 tsp) orange curaçao
20ml (¾fl oz) AE Dor Cognac
100ml (3½fl oz) NV champagne
1 small spoon of good-quality vanilla ice cream

Add all the ingredients except the champagne and ice cream to a mixing glass with ice. Stir, then strain into a chilled coupe and top up with the champagne. Add a scoop of ice cream on top and serve immediately.

Bartender's Tip
For an alternative take, add the spoon of ice cream first. Shake the other ingredients except the champagne with ice, then strain over the ice cream. Top with champagne and serve it as a foaming cup.

Champagne Sorbet

This is somewhere between a canapé and a cocktail, and is a particularly sophisticated, gourmet way to approach champagne. The delicate flavour of the caviar and the silky sweet hazelnut aromas are offset by the freshness of the champagne sorbet. This is a perfect companion for a chic start to a fine dining experience.

GLASSWARE
Coupe

ICE
None

GARNISH
None

SERVES 1

2 tsp homemade champagne sorbet (*see* below)
1 tsp caviar
Hazelnut essence

For the champagne sorbet
(Makes 300ml/½ pint)
375g (12oz) caster sugar
45g (2oz) glucose
325ml (11fl oz) mineral water
1 lemon
750ml (1¼ pints) ultra brut champagne
½ tsp baking powder

Bartender's Tip
For an extra citrus hit, add the juice of half a fresh grapefruit to the sorbet at the same stage as the lemon juice.

To make the champagne sorbet it is best to use an ice cream machine, if possible. First, make a syrup. Put the sugar, glucose and mineral water in a saucepan and bring to the boil. Remove from the heat, stir in a squeeze of lemon juice and leave to cool. This syrup can be stored in the refrigerator until needed. When cold, measure out 300ml (½ pint) of the syrup and mix with the champagne, baking powder and the juice of half a lemon. Pour everything into the ice cream machine and freeze according to the manufacturer's instructions. Once made, store in a freezer.

Remove the sorbet from the freezer just prior to serving. Add 2 teaspoons of sorbet to a coupe, top with the caviar, then spritz with hazelnut essence from an atomizer. Serve immediately.

Sgroppino No.2

The Sgroppino is traditionally used as a palate cleanser between courses during formal dinners in Italy. The bitter sourness of the sorbet refreshes the palate and, along with the Amaro Lucano liqueur, represents two flavours so reminiscent of southern Italy. The cocoa beans add dryness to the mix, the vodka elegantly bridges the flavours, while the champagne adds a delightful fruitiness. Finally, the tonka bean adds a scent of vanilla and spice.

GLASSWARE
Wine

ICE
Cubes to shake, none to serve

GARNISH
Grated tonka bean, lemon twist

SERVES 1

15ml (½fl oz) Konik's Tail vodka
10ml (2 tsp) Amaro Lucano infusion (*see* below)
5ml (1 tsp) black cardamom syrup (*see* below)
50ml (1¾fl oz) vintage champagne

For the Amaro Lucano infusion
250g (8oz) cocoa beans
750ml (1¼ pints) Amaro Lucano

For the black cardamom syrup
70g (3oz) black cardamom pods
1 litre (1¾ pints) sugar syrup

Bartender's Tip
When it comes to infusions, the general rule of thumb is that delicate ingredients (such as raspberries and cinnamon sticks) will take less time to infuse. For stronger ingredients (such as cocoa beans) you can use stronger spirits.

First make the Amaro Lucano infusion. Crush the cocoa beans in a pestle and mortar, then add them to a container filled with the bottle of Amaro Lucano. Leave to infuse for a minimum of 6–8 hours, then strain and bottle in a sterilized container.

Next make the syrup. Slit the cardamom pods and extract the seeds. Pour the sugar syrup into a bowl, add the cardamom skins and seeds and use an electric hand mixer to blend together. Leave to infuse for 5 hours, then strain and bottle in a sterilized container.

To make the cocktail, add all the ingredients except the champagne to a shaker with ice. Shake well, then double strain (see page 219) into a wine glass and top up with the champagne. Garnish with grated tonka bean and a lemon twist. Serve immediately.

Mexican Chic

This is the essence of Mexico in a glass, with an added touch of sophistication from the rosé champagne. The fresh green fruit fragrance and peppery notes of the tequila are mellowed by the aromatic syrup and balanced by the lime. The rosé champagne complements the different flavours to create the ultimate revitalizing cocktail.

GLASSWARE
Highball

ICE
Cubes to shake and to serve

GARNISH
None

SERVES 1

30ml (1fl oz) Jose Cuervo Tradicional reposado tequila
15ml (½fl oz) lime juice
15ml (½fl oz) hibiscus syrup (*see* Bartender's Tip)
120ml (4fl oz) NV rosé champagne

Bartender's Tip
You can buy hibiscus flowers in syrup, but to make at home, steep 100g (3½oz) hibiscus flowers in 1 litre (1¾ pints) boiling water for 7 minutes. Strain, then use the infused water to make a flavoured sugar syrup (see page 220).

Add all the ingredients except the champagne to a shaker with ice. Shake well, then double strain (*see* page 219) into a highball glass over ice and top up with the champagne.

Moonwalk

One of London's most famous cocktails, the Moonwalk was conceived in 1969 by Joe Gilmore, head barman at The Savoy hotel's American Bar in London, to commemorate the first time humans landed on the Moon. Legend has it that it was the first drink that Neil Armstrong and Buzz Aldrin enjoyed on returning to Earth. Combining grapefruit juice, orange liqueur and a touch of rosewater, topped with champagne, it has the perfect balance between citrus freshness and a full-bodied spirit. The Moonwalk is the ultimate celebration cocktail.

GLASSWARE
Flute

ICE
Cubes to shake, none to serve

GARNISH
Orange twist

SERVES 1

25ml (¾fl oz) Grand Marnier
25ml (¾fl oz) grapefruit juice
4 drops of rosewater
100ml (3½fl oz) NV champagne

Add all the ingredients except the champagne to a shaker with ice. Shake well, then strain into a chilled flute and top up with the champagne. Garnish with an orange twist.

Bartender's Tip
With most cocktails, it is recommended that for the best results you should always try to keep your glasses in a freezer as the ultra-chilled glass will allow the drink to stay cold for longer.

Hidden Gem

In this elegant cocktail, the liqueurs lift and enhance the aromatic, fruity and tannic aromas of the Armagnac, while the champagne adds crispness and helps the flavours to develop as you drink it. The name is taken from the crystallized stem ginger that is almost imperceptible at the bottom of the glass. The fine bubbles of the champagne impart its subtle flavour, bringing another level of sophistication to the drink.

GLASSWARE
Flute

ICE
Cubes to stir, none to serve

GARNISH
Crystallized ginger cube,
lemon twist (discarded)

SERVES 1

25ml (¾fl oz) Darroze
   Armagnac 20yo
5ml (1 tsp) Bols honey liqueur
2.5ml (½ tsp) orange curaçao
Vintage rosé champagne,
   to top up

Bartender's Tip
If you want to give this cocktail a sweeter, spicier kick, add a teaspoon or two of the crystalized ginger syrup.

Add the Armagnac, honey liqueur and curaçao to a mixing glass with ice and stir gently. Place the crystallized ginger in a chilled flute. Strain the cocktail into the flute, then top up with champagne. Zest the lemon twist to release the oils over the surface of the drink (see page 219), then discard the twist.

1852 Fizz

Boodles gin is one of my favourites as it has such a distinctive, aromatic flavour with sweet spices and zesty, rooty notes, too. In this loose take on a classic Gin Fizz, the gin's juniper and citrus botanicals are lifted by the lime juice, while the lemon verbena tea syrup adds a smoothness and a more subtle lemony flavour. Ginseng has a certain woodiness to it and then the champagne brings all the flavours together. Finally, the subtly bitter caramelized kumquat imparts an extra layer of flavour.

GLASSWARE
Wine

ICE
Cubes to throw, none to serve

GARNISH
Caramelized kumquat (*see* method)

SERVES 1

30ml (1fl oz) Boodles gin
20ml (¾fl oz) lemon verbena syrup (*see* below)
10ml (2 tsp) lime juice
3 drops of ginseng essence
100ml (3½fl oz) NV champagne

For the lemon verbena syrup (Serves 12)
25g (1oz) dried lemon verbena leaves
250ml (8fl oz) cold water

For the caramelized kumquats
1kg (2lb) fresh kumquats
150g (5oz) juniper berries
1 litre (1¾ pints) sugar syrup

> *Bartender's Tip*
> Ginseng essence is available as an oral liquid from health food shops and online retailers. It is a natural tonic that improves memory, concentration and overall well-being.

If you want to serve this cocktail as designed, here's how to caramelize kumquats: puncture the skins of the kumquats with a cocktail stick or skewer. Place the kumquats in a saucepan of water and bring to the boil. Drain, add fresh water and boil again twice more to extract the bitterness from the fruit. Make a juniper-flavoured syrup (created by infusing the juniper berries in warm sugar syrup). Transfer the kumquats to a sterilized jar and top up with the syrup to cover. Store in a cool place for 4 weeks until caramelized.

To make the lemon verbena syrup, steep the dried lemon verbena leaves in the cold water for 2 hours. Strain, then combine one part sugar to one part infused water and stir until the sugar has dissolved.

To make the cocktail, add all the ingredients except the champagne to a shaker with ice. Throw the mixture from one shaker to another to aerate and chill the drink. Add the champagne and stir, then double strain into a chilled wine glass. Garnish with a caramelized kumquat.

MODERNIST COCKTAILS

'Candy is dandy,
but liquor is quicker.'
Ogden Nash, Hard Lines

Recipes by Thomas Aske

The Worship Street Whistling Shop, London

Modernist Cocktails
by Paul Henderson

Molecular mixology. Progressive bartending. Modernist cocktails. Alcoholic alchemy. However you choose to brand the contemporary art of using scientific equipment and techniques to create spectacular drinking 'experiences', there is no disputing that the process has taken the concept of cocktail-making to a new level. A mixture of sensory exploration, vaudeville theatre and chemical masterclass, at their best they can completely change your conception of what a drink can be. At their worst, though...well, let's just say if you play with liquid nitrogen you can get burned.

To understand the method behind the madness of the modernist cocktail, it is necessary to go back to the origins of molecular gastronomy – a school of cooking that its main proponents say doesn't even exist. Confused? You will be.

In 1992, French chemist Hervé This, Oxford physicist Nicholas Kurti and American food science writer Harold McGee organized a workshop in Italy to discuss and investigate science and its role in cooking techniques (roasting, boiling, braising, etc). Originally, they had planned to call their seminar Science & Gastronomy, but at some point that was altered to Molecular Gastronomy.

By the late-1990s, a new generation of chefs began experimenting with scientific principles in their recipes, principally Spain's Ferran Adrià, France's Pierre Gagnaire and Britain's Heston Blumenthal. Through exploration and investigation, the chefs came together with the scientists, and by sharing information the molecular gastronomy label was quickly applied to their cooking. The title stuck but the key exponents disagreed with what the name implied. They were not mad scientists, they maintained. They were just chefs applying very modern methods to classic cooking principles. 'I wasn't against the term molecular gastronomy per se, but I was opposed to what that description had come to mean and to what cooking it was applied to,' says Blumenthal. 'A few years ago, a few of us got together to discuss the type of cuisine we were creating and to make a statement on our "new" cookery. And what we decided was that this cookery should be applied to every form of cooking, from a cup of coffee to a 15-course tasting menu...as a result, I do have a much more emotional attachment to the modernist cuisine description.'

In the course of their experiments, the chefs began utilizing Cryovac machines (to vacuum-seal ingredients), sous-vide machines (water ovens for cooking at very low temperatures), and Pacojets (to micro-purée foods to make ice creams and sorbets); and cooking with liquid nitrogen (for flash freezing), hydrocolloids (to produce gels), among others. It was only a matter of time before inquisitive mixologists got in on the act.

In New York, the man considered one of the pioneers of modernist bartending is Eben Freeman. Already a ten-year cocktail veteran, in 2003 Freeman teamed up with modernist chef Wylie Dufresne at wd~50, then worked bar at Tailor and began pushing the cocktail envelope. Freeman, too, dislikes the molecular tag, preferring 'progressive cocktails' as a description for his work, but his creations – smoked Coca-Cola, a frozen mango Daiquiri with chilli

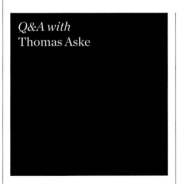
How did you get into the business? Initially I worked collecting glasses to earn some money while studying, before falling in love with the social element of the job.

What is your bartending philosophy? The guest should always be the priority. The bartender should provide the guest with a bespoke and genuine service that has them leaving feeling like the most important person in the room.

Who was your mentor/ bartending inspiration? My first bar manager Jason Tank: he taught me the foundations of being a good bartender, how to make classic cocktails and also the fun side to the job.

What is your favourite cocktail ingredient at the moment? Definitely our own Whistling Shop Acid Phosphate. It offers a third dimension to mixed drinks.

What is your favourite bar in the world, and why? Cafe No Se in Antigua, Guatamala. It's the perfect blend of dive-bar-meets-traditional-tavern. The best part of it is their mezcal bar – mezcal and beer, two shots minimum, as they exclaim on the door.

What would be the cocktail you would drink on your deathbed... and who would make it? Bit of a strange one, but if it could be anyone alive or dead, then a Sazerac from Ian Fleming would be a pretty good way to go.

syrup, and his infamous 'solid cocktails' (gin-and-tonic jellies and absinthe Gummi Bears) – pointed mixologists in a new direction. 'You can really play with people's preconceptions,' Freeman says. 'For example, imagine the most sublime Black Russian you've ever had, but as a crystal-clear liquid. Instead of having set cocktails, you can start with an idea about a flavour and then think how you'd use it in an ideal world. You can really push the boundaries.'

In London, Tony Conigliaro – who came up with the legendary No.5 Champagne Cocktail that had a Chanel perfume aroma – is considered the UK's progressive cocktail guru. Having developed his skills at Isola and the Shochu Lounge, Conigliaro currently runs his own bar, 69 Colebrooke Row, otherwise known as The Bar With No Name. He can also be found in the Drink Factory, his libation laboratory where he and a few like-minded bartenders work on ideas, experiment with flavours and ingredients, and generally act as futurist alcohol apothecaries. Heston Blumenthal, who collaborated with Conigliaro on a cocktail menu at his restaurant The Fat Duck, describes him simply as 'a revolutionary'. 'For years and years all we'd ever had is recipes passed down. You'd get shown how to make them and shown what they should be like and how they should taste,' says Conigliaro, who is also a *GQ* cocktail columnist. 'But it was scratching below the surface of that and seeing what was actually going on that really proved to be of interest for us.'

Following in Conigliaro's footsteps are world-renowned mixologists Tristan Stephenson and *GQ Drinks'* Thomas Aske, co-owners of the Worship Street Whistling Shop and the Fluid Movement bar-consultancy company. Making drinking an immersive experience, their cellar bar serves original and spectacular cocktails in the setting of a Victorian-gothic gin palace, complete with a dram shop and a glass-walled laboratory. For Aske, it is a logical extension to enjoying a cocktail. By feeding into all your senses – the sights, the smells, the sounds, the atmosphere – you will get so much more from your cocktail than just a tasty beverage. And they do make very, very tasty beverages. For example, the Black Cat's Martini is made with gin that has been infused with cream and sugar...but then the cream is removed so that the spirit remains perfectly clear. If it weren't modernist, you'd call it witchcraft. It is so good, they will even sell you a bottle of their patented Cream Gin so you can make it at home. 'At the Whistling Shop we take a multisensory approach to drinking,' says Aske. 'Each element of our cocktails is given consideration for its aroma, flavour combination and delivery. Our guests' senses are challenged through our use of modernist techniques such as sous-vide cooked shrubs, nitrogen cavitation infusions or homemade tinctures created on the rotary evaporator. When a guest enters the Whistling Shop they are guided through and welcomed to this way of experimental drinking, and when they leave, they feel mesmerized, empowered and inspired.'

And you thought the only choice was shaken or stirred. A word of warning, however: if you do attempt some of Aske's daring drinks, just remember not to call it molecular mixology!

Cold Buttered Flip

This modern interpretation of the classic 17th-century tavern and sailors' beverage starts with butterfat-washed Diplomático Reserva Exclusiva rum. Fat-washing the rum leads to a soft, creamy and velvety finish that enhances the additional ingredients to provide a further layer of taste. Original flips consisted of beer, rum and sugar that would have been heated with a red-hot poker called a loggerhead. All too often these loggerheads would also be used to settle disputes among guests, which led to the expression 'to be at loggerheads'.

GLASSWARE
Toby jug

ICE
Hand-carved to shake, none to serve

GARNISH
Dehydrated banana fruit leather (see method), liquorice root, lavender, burned cinnamon

SERVES 1

50ml (1¾fl oz) butterfat-washed rum (see below)
15ml (½fl oz) fig liqueur
15ml (½fl oz) stout
1 dash of Butterfly absinthe
20ml (¾fl oz) sugar syrup
1 egg

For the banana fruit leather (Serves 6–8)
2 overripe bananas
10ml (2 tsp) sugar syrup
5ml (1 tsp) lemon juice

For the butterfat-washed rum (Makes 700ml/1¼ pints)
1 (700ml/1¼ pint) bottle Diplomático Reserva Exclusiva rum
190g (7oz) unsalted butter

You will also need
Dehydrator
Milk frother

To make the banana fruit leather for the garnish, purée the bananas in a blender or food processor, then add the sugar syrup and lemon juice. Spread the banana purée thinly on a dehydrator tray lined with baking paper. Place in a dehydrator for about 3 hours or until the banana begins to become firm. Turn the banana over on the tray and dehydrate for a further 1 hour or until firm. Alternatively, to make the banana leather in a conventional oven, set the oven to its lowest setting and cook for around 3 hours.

To make the butterfat-washed rum, pour 525ml (18fl oz) of the rum into a large plastic container with a lid. Melt the butter in a saucepan over a low heat and pour into the rum. Seal the container, then shake and place in the freezer overnight. When frozen, strain to remove the butter solids. Cut the butterfat-washed rum with the remaining rum that has not been fat-washed.

To make the cocktail, put all the cocktail ingredients in a mixing tin and whisk with a milk frother for 30 seconds. Add ice and shake hard until the tin is frosted. Strain into a toby jug and garnish with the banana fruit leather, liquorice root, lavender and burned cinnamon (cinnamon sprinkled over a flame).

Claro Fandango

Taking a playful nudge from the tequila and cola consumed in Mexico and the Mexican penchant for toasted insects, this beverage utilizes a home-made, salted clear cola tablet that creates the flavour of cola. By adjusting the flavours and quantities of the oils used in it, you can develop a variety of different-flavoured tablets. The sweetened tequila and water are then poured over, releasing the flavour and generating effervescence from the bicarbonate of soda at the same time. The beverage is served with a toasted scorpion and edible olive-oil sand.

GLASSWARE
Bottle, ceramic pot

ICE
None

GARNISH
Edible olive-oil sand (*see* method), toasted edible scorpion/insect

SERVES 1

50ml (1¾fl oz) Tapatio Blanco tequila
4 dashes of acid phosphate
15ml (½fl oz) agave nectar
75ml (2½fl oz) water
1 salted cola tablet (*see* below)

For the edible olive-oil sand
50g (2oz) maltodextrin
50ml (1¾fl oz) olive oil
1 tsp salt

For the salted cola tablet (Makes 1)
40g (1½oz) dextrose
15g (½oz) bicarbonate of soda
15g (½oz) citric acid
½ tsp salt
1 drop of orange oil
1 drop of lime oil
¼ tsp cassia oil
¼ tsp lemon oil
1 drop of nutmeg oil
1 drop of neroli oil
1 drop of lavender oil
10ml (2 tsp) water

To make the olive-oil sand, put the maltodextrin, olive oil and salt in a food mixer and mix on a medium speed until the maltodextrin has absorbed the olive oil. To produce a fine sand, gently sieve the mixture. Store in an airtight container.

To make the salted cola tablet, put all the tablet ingredients except the water in a food mixer and mix on a low speed. Slowly add the water until the mixture binds together. Press the powder into a 25ml (1fl oz) jelly or chocolate mould and compact it until it can hold its shape. Gently press the tablet out of the mould.

To make the cocktail, place all the ingredients except the tablet in a bottle; cork it and then refrigerate. Place the cola tablet in a ceramic pot. When the liquid is well chilled, pour the bottled solution over the cola tablet and stir. Garnish with the edible olive-oil sand and toasted edible scorpion/insect to serve.

The Exciseman

Harking back to illicit spirit production of the 18th century, The Exciseman takes inspiration from the smoke plumes billowing from moonshine stills in the Scottish Highlands. The ingredients bring together the maritime flavours of the coastal highlands and the sweetness of heather honey from Speyside. The components of this digestif are rested in sherry stave barrels to add complexities of raisins, dates and figs (all key flavours found in Bruichladdich Islay single malt Scotch whisky). Gently smoking the inside of the glass with anise provides theatre while enhancing the complexity of the cocktail.

GLASSWARE
Rocks

ICE
None

GARNISH
Whisky-cured blue cheese (*see* method), smoked star anise

MAKES A 1-LITRE BARREL

570ml (1 pint) Bruichladdich 10yo Islay single malt Scotch whisky
215ml (7½fl oz) oloroso sherry
215ml (7½fl oz) muscovado sugar syrup (*see* below)
3ml (½ tsp) salted water

For the muscovado sugar syrup (Makes 250ml/8fl oz)
250ml (8fl oz) water
250g (9oz) muscovado sugar

For the whisky-cured blue cheese (Serves 20)
500ml (18fl oz) Bruichladdich 10yo Islay single malt Scotch whisky
500g (1lb) Stilton cheese, cut into cubes

To make the syrup, put the water and sugar in a saucepan and heat until the sugar has dissolved, then leave to cool. Bottle in a sterilized container and refrigerate until ready to use.

To 'barrel-age' the cocktail, put all the cocktail ingredients in a 1 litre (1¾ pint) European oak barrel and leave to mature for 2–4 weeks. The ageing process will serve to mellow the cocktail and allow the ingredients to marry while adding the aroma and flavour of dried fruit. Taste the cocktail regularly while it is in the barrel to ensure that it is not over-ageing.

To make the whisky-cured blue cheese for the garnish, put the whisky and the cubed cheese in an airtight container, cover and allow to macerate overnight.

To complete the cocktail, place the star anise on a heatproof surface and use a chef's blowtorch to heat it until it begins to smoke. Place a rocks glass over the anise to capture the smoke and infuse the inside of the glass. After 5 seconds, turn the glass over, releasing the smoke, and add the barrel-aged cocktail to the glass. Garnish with the whisky-cured blue cheese and smoked star anise.

Hop & Rigour

The distinctive anchor on a bottle of Veuve Clicquot is the Christian symbol for hope and rigour, inspiring this cocktail's name and its subtle twist. Veuve Clicquot's key aromatics of vanilla, biscuit, brioche, pear, anise and peach are accentuated using homemade Butterfly absinthe and vanilla candyfloss, atomized with hop-infused pear eau de vie. This drink takes all of the elegance of early 20th-century Paris and fuses it with a modern pairing. The delicate candyfloss gives a taste of sweetness, and this flavour will coat the palate before being washed by the dryness and subtle citrus found in the champagne.

GLASSWARE
Flute

ICE
None

GARNISH
Absinthe and vanilla candyfloss (*see* method), atomizer containing hop-infused pear eau de vie (*see* below), edible rice-paper butterfly

SERVES 1

175ml Veuve Clicquot Yellow Label champagne

For the absinthe and vanilla candyfloss
250g (8oz) caster sugar
1 vanilla pod, halved
10ml (2 tsp) Butterfly absinthe

For the hop-infused pear eau de vie
200ml (7fl oz) pear eau de vie
100g (3½oz) hops

You will also need
Candyfloss machine
1 food-grade wooden candyfloss stick
Atomizer

To make the hop-infused pear eau de vie, mix the pear eau de vie and the hops together in an airtight container and leave to infuse for 24 hours. Strain through a fine sieve and decant into the atomizer.

To make the absinthe and vanilla candyfloss, place the candyfloss ingredients in an airtight container and leave to infuse overnight. Preheat the candyfloss machine. Place a measure of the infused sugar into the machine and spin to form the candyfloss.

To serve the cocktail, pour the champagne into a chilled flute. Spray the candyfloss with the hop-infused pear eau de vie, garnish with an edible paper butterfly (if using) and serve alongside the champagne.

The Devil's Toll

In the American whiskey industry, the gentle ageing process inevitably leads to the evaporation and loss of alcohol from the cask. This loss is usually called 'the angels' share' but in some places it is known as 'the devil's toll'. The Devil's Toll cocktail uses a homemade vanilla cola to create a drink that is both simple and complex, accentuating the characteristics of the Gentleman Jack Rare Tennessee whiskey. The theatre of this drink is added through the use of flash paper currency that has been atomized with cedar wood, an aroma that will be released when the 'toll' is lit.

GLASSWARE
Ceramic barrel mug

ICE
Hand-carved to serve

GARNISH
Flash paper currency sprayed with cedar-wood essence, dried orange slice, fresh mint leaves

SERVES 1

250ml (9fl oz) homemade vanilla cola syrup (*see* below)
750ml (1¼ pints) water
50ml (1¾fl oz) Gentleman Jack Rare Tennessee whiskey
1 dash of chocolate bitters

For the homemade vanilla cola syrup (Makes 1.2 litres/2 pints)
500ml (18fl oz) water
500g (1lb) caster sugar
Grated zest of **2** oranges, **1** lemon and **1** lime
5ml (1 tsp) ground coriander
5ml (1 tsp) dried lavender
1 star anise
2 vanilla pods
1 cinnamon stick
1.5ml (¼ tsp) citric acid powder

You will also need
Soda siphon and **2** carbon dioxide charges
Atomizer

To make the syrup, put all the syrup ingredients in a large saucepan and simmer for 15 minutes. Strain through muslin and leave to cool. Bottle in a sterilized container and refrigerate until ready to use.

To make the cocktail, put 250ml (8fl oz) of the cola syrup and the water in a soda siphon. Charge with 2 carbon dioxide canisters and refrigerate. After 2 hours, pour the whiskey into a mug over ice, add the bitters and top up with the homemade cola from the siphon. Spray the flash paper currency with cedar-wood essence from an atomizer and attach to the vessel. Garnish with a dried orange slice and mint leaves. When ready to serve, light the flash paper. This will release the aroma designed as the final garnish for the beverage.

The Enlightened Botanist

The Enlightened Botanist fuses and modernizes the Negroni and the G&T by using a bitter Campari jelly to accompany the delicate floral beverage. The Botanist Islay Dry gin is distilled in a small copper pot still and so this drink is garnished with a juniper oil burner, representing the aromas one would experience in a still room. The presentation and delivery of a cocktail can have a bold impact on the overall experience and can help tell a story. In this instance, the copper-still oil burner gives a practical example of how gin is produced while at the same time adding aromatics to the cocktail.

GLASSWARE
Thin-sided rocks, small glasses or jelly moulds

ICE
Cubes to stir, hand-carved to serve

GARNISH
Bitter grapefruit jelly (*see* method), dried orange or grapefruit slice, juniper oil

SERVES 1

40ml (1¼fl oz) The Botanist Islay Dry gin
20ml (¾fl oz) Martini Rosso
5ml (1 tsp) heather honey syrup (*see* below)
3 dashes of Bob's coriander bitters

For the bitter grapefruit jelly (Makes 10)
4 gelatine leaves
400ml (14fl oz) pink grapefruit juice
75ml (2½fl oz) sugar syrup
25ml (¾fl oz) Campari

For the heather honey syrup (Makes 300ml/½ pint)
125ml (4fl oz) water
250g (8oz) heather honey

You will also need
Oil burner and tealight

To make the bitter grapefruit jelly, soak the gelatine leaves in cold water for 5 minutes. Put the grapefruit juice, sugar syrup and Campari in a small saucepan and heat gently to just short of boiling. Drain the gelatine leaves and add to the pan, whisking to dissolve. Pour into 50ml (1³/₄fl oz) jelly moulds, small glasses or other suitable vessels and refrigerate. Leave to set.

To make the syrup, gently heat the water until just short of boiling point. Add the heather honey and stir to dissolve. Leave to cool. Bottle in a sterilized container and refrigerate until ready to use.

To make the cocktail, put all the cocktail ingredients in a mixing glass with ice. Stir gently until chilled, then strain into a rocks glass over carved ice. Garnish with the dried orange slice. Put 2 drops of juniper oil in the oil burner and light, then serve with the cocktail and the bitter grapefruit jelly.

The Baker's Cup

The inspiration for this drink came from the complex and unusual flavour profile of Belvedere Unfiltered vodka. Freshly baked bread, white pepper and vanilla are balanced with floral notes of elderflower and sweetly acidic peach from the Riesling. The key to this cocktail is that it manages to excite all of the senses, with the introduction of the detonated balloon garnish adding the aroma of freshly baked bread. Flash string can be purchased online or from any good magicians' shop.

GLASSWARE
Coupe

ICE
Cubes to stir, none to serve

GARNISH
Baked bread essence balloon

SERVES 1

Loose green tea
Finely grated zest of **1** lemon
50ml (1¾fl oz) Belvedere Unfiltered vodka
20ml (¾fl oz) Riesling
10ml (2 tsp) elderflower cordial
1 dash of Bob's peppermint bitters

You will also need
Tea diffuser
Baked bread essence
Balloon
Helium
Flash string

Fill the tea diffuser with loose green tea and grated lemon zest. Put 2 drops of baked bread essence into the balloon and fill with helium; tie to close. Attach the flash string to the balloon and connect to the tea diffuser.

Add the vodka, Riesling, elderflower cordial and bitters to a mixing glass with ice. Stir until chilled, then strain into a coupe glass. Place the tea diffuser into the glass and leave to macerate. When ready to serve, light the flash string near the end and allow it to burn to the balloon. This will result in the balloon detonating over the glass, dispersing the baked bread aroma over the drink.

Clouded Horizon

The deep, rich characteristics of the 23-year-old Guatemalan rum used in this cocktail conjure images of the mountains surrounding the region of Antigua Guatemala. Horseback riding through the mountains can be thirsty work, so we designed this beverage for a hip flask to provide light relief, using one of the world's greatest rums as its base. The key flavours contained in the Ron Zacapa 23 rum allow for the delicate use of Picon Bière, with its caramelized orange and citrus notes, and a bitter IPA syrup. The drink is lightened with Dr Adam Elmegirab's dandelion & burdock bitters.

GLASSWARE
Hip flask, cigar box

ICE
Cubes to stir, none to serve

GARNISH
Chocolate cigars, salted liquorice foam (*see* method)

SERVES 1

50ml (1¾fl oz) Ron Zacapa 23 rum
20ml (¾fl oz) Picon Bière bitters
10ml (2 tsp) IPA syrup (*see* below)
3 dashes of Dr Adam Elmegirab's dandelion & burdock bitters

For the salted liquorice foam (Serves 20)
6 gelatine leaves
750ml (1¼ pints) apple juice
200g (7oz) liquorice tea
1 pinch of salt

For the IPA syrup (Makes 500ml/18fl oz)
500ml (18fl oz) Indian Pale Ale
500g (1lb) caster sugar

You will also need
Cream whipper and **2** nitrous oxide charges

To make the salted liquorice foam, soak the gelatine leaves in cold water for 5 minutes. Put the apple juice, tea and salt in a saucepan and heat gently to just short of boiling point. Strain away the tea. Drain the gelatine leaves and add to the pan, whisking to dissolved. Put the liquid in a cream whipper and screw the lid on. Charge with 2 nitrous oxide canisters and shake. Refrigerate for 2 hours before dispensing.

To make the syrup, put the IPA in a saucepan and heat gently to just short of boiling point. Add the sugar and simmer for 10 minutes, then leave to cool. Bottle in a sterilized container and refrigerate until ready to use.

To make the cocktail, add all the cocktail ingredients to a mixing glass with ice. Stir, then strain through a fine sieve into a hip flask. Serve with chocolate cigars and the salted liquorice foam.

L'Hermione's Scent

L'Hermione's Scent is named after and inspired by the famous French ship L'Hermione, which ferried General Lafayette to America in 1780. Both the general and the ship were involved in fighting against the British in the American War of Independence. The Hennessy Fine de Cognac has subtle aromatics of fresh mango and a floral finesse, and so the use of a bespoke 'shrub' in this cocktail leads to a heightened experience of the Cognac. A shrub is a vinegar-based drink derived from the centuries-old practice of using vinegar to preserve fruit.

GLASSWARE
Egg cup

ICE
Cubes to shake, none to serve

GARNISH
Dried lemon slice, fizzy grapes (*see* method), hibiscus flower (optional)

SERVES 1

50ml (1¾fl oz) Hennessy Fine de Cognac
15ml (½fl oz) mango and hibiscus shrub
25ml (¾fl oz) lemon juice
20ml (¾fl oz) eucalyptus honey
1 egg white

For the mango and hibiscus shrub (Makes 500ml/18fl oz)
500ml (18fl oz) cider vinegar
250g (8oz) ripe mango, finely sliced
250g (8oz) hibiscus flowers
250g (8oz) caster sugar

For the fizzy grapes
1 bunch of grapes

You will also need
Soda siphon and **2** carbon dioxide canisters
Milk frother

To make the mango and hibiscus shrub, put all the shrub ingredients in an airtight container. Leave to macerate for 5 days or until the sugar has dissolved. Strain the liquid through muslin, pressing the remaining juice from the mango. Bottle in a sterilized container and refrigerate until ready to use.

To make the fizzy grapes, put the grapes in a soda siphon and screw on the lid. Charge with 2 carbon dioxide canisters, then refrigerate for 24 hours. Dispense the gas from the siphon before unscrewing the lid. Empty the now fizzy grapes and use immediately (they will only remain fizzy for about an hour).

To make the cocktail, put all the cocktail ingredients in a Boston tin and whisk with a milk frother for 30 seconds. Add ice and shake vigorously until chilled. Strain into an egg cup. Garnish with a dried lemon slice, fizzy grapes and an hibiscus flower (if using).

THE
LONDON
PECULIARS
fog cutter

Originality: Victorian Gentlemans Club
Provenance & Period: London 1837
Aroma Description: Sill Room, Orchid & Meadow
Blossom
Style Description: Social Lubricant

VINE STREET
LONDON

IMPRO
EARTHEN
IN HA
MANUFACTU
BY
S. MAW, SON &
LIMITED
ALDERSCATE St. LONDON
ENGLAND

London Peculiars

In London, the Victorian era saw an emergence of pharmaceutical remedies for common ailments caused by the smog, also known as the London Peculiars. As many of the ailments involved respiratory problems, this beverage is served with a Victorian inhaler dispensing a camomile dry-ice 'fog'. The delicate aromas of Tanqueray No. TEN gin are balanced by clarified apple juice and rhubarb syrup and acid phosphate. Because a green drink can automatically be associated with apple, removing this colour leaves the interpretation open to the individual.

GLASSWARE
Pharmacy bottle

ICE
None

GARNISH
Camomile tea dry-ice 'fog'

SERVES 1

50ml (1¾fl oz) Tanqueray No. TEN gin
50ml (1¾fl oz) clarified apple juice (*see below*)
15ml (½fl oz) clarified rhubarb syrup (*see below*)
3 dashes of acid phosphate
20ml (¾fl oz) water

For the clarified apple juice
(Makes 500ml/18fl oz)
750g (1½lb) cold apple juice
1.5g (¼ tsp) agar (0.2 per cent of total juice weight)

For the clarified rhubarb syrup
(Makes 450ml/16fl oz)
100g (3½oz) sliced rhubarb
750ml (1¼ pints) water
1.5g (¼ tsp) agar
750g (1½lb) caster sugar

You will also need
Inhaler
Dry ice
Hot camomile tea

To make the clarified apple juice, divide up the apple juice and chill 250g (8oz) and 500g (1lb) separately. Whisk the agar into the 250g (8oz) cold apple juice until fully dispersed, then pour into a large saucepan and bring to the boil. Add the 500g (1lb) cold apple juice, whisking vigorously and taking care not to let the mixture cool too quickly. Place over an ice bath to cool and set. Once set, use a whisk to break up the curds. Place the curds in a muslin-lined chinois (a fine-meshed conical sieve) and squeeze to drain the clarified liquid, then refrigerate until ready to use.

To make the clarified rhubarb syrup, put the sliced rhubarb and water in a saucepan and bring to the boil, then reduce the heat and simmer for 15 minutes. Strain, then press the liquid through a muslin cloth to extract the juice. Leave the liquid to separate naturally for 20 minutes before gently decanting the pink juice, then refrigerate until ready to use. Once cool, measure 500g (1lb) and 250g (8oz) of the rhubarb juice. Whisk the agar into the 250g (8oz) rhubarb juice until fully dispersed, then pour into a large saucepan and bring to the boil. Slowly pour the 500g (1lb) rhubarb juice into the pan taking care not to cool the solution below 30°C (86°F). Place over an ice bath to cool and set. Once set, use a whisk to break up the curds. Place the curds in a muslin-lined chinois and squeeze to drain the clarified liquid, which will have a light pink hue. Add the sugar to the clarified rhubarb juice and leave to dissolve, shaking the mixture occasionally. Bottle in a sterilized container and refrigerate until ready to use.

To make the cocktail, add all the cocktail ingredients to a pharmacy bottle and refrigerate until ready to serve. Put a small scoop of dry ice into the Victorian inhaler, then pour over a strongly brewed camomile tea. Serve with the cocktail.

CLASSIC & SPECIALIST

COCKTAILS & SPIRITS

'What difference is there
between a glass of absinthe
and a sunset?'
Oscar Wilde

Recipes by Simone Caporale

Artesian, The Langham, London

Classic Cocktails
& Specialist Spirits
by Amy Matthews

If gin, rum, vodka and whisky are the main building blocks of a bar or drinks cabinet, then it is the bottles of vermouth, bitters and liqueurs that are the finishing touches. They transform cocktails from a mere assembly of spirits in a glass to a drink of balance and beauty.

BITTERS The Ancient Egyptians and Greeks first dissolved herbs and spices in a high-strength alcohol for their supposed medicinal side effects. While the modern bartender turns to the same techniques purely for the taste sensation, the pharmaceutical roots of aromatic bitters are more influential than you might think. Adam McGurk, bar manager at London's Hawksmoor Air Street, says that many of the restorative cocktails on their list would originally have been drunk for pain relief rather than pleasure. 'Peychaud's bitters were created around 1830 by the famous apothecary Antoine Peychaud. They were used to create the Sazerac, which almost certainly would have been perceived as medicinal. At that time, alcohol was still the primary vessel for medicine, capturing the curative qualities of herbs, barks and botanicals.'

Aromatic bitters now prove their worth by adding the necessary historic touch to modern interpretations of pre-Prohibition classics. 'It is a way of squeezing quite an intense amount of flavour into a drink without adding a lot of liquid,' says Adam. 'They act like a bridging ingredient sometimes, filling in little gaps. Even though they can have quite big, bitter, spicy flavours, they can help mellow the flavour of a drink.' Angostura bitters remain the most ubiquitous – essential in many classics, from a Champagne Cocktail to a Manhattan, they embody the concentrated complexity that a dash can bring to an otherwise two-dimensional drink.

Italy took inspiration from the original Roman bitters and tinctures and turned them into some of the most enduring aperitifs and digestifs. Of the former, Campari and Aperol are still popular, loosened with soda water or prosecco. They have also become increasingly popular in considerably colder climes, as Northern palates have become more attuned to Italian tastes in food and wine.

Digestive bitters are an entirely different proposition. Best enjoyed at the end of a lengthy and indulgent dinner, their resemblance to cough syrup is quickly forgotten as the herbal ingredients work their magic on poor, abused internal organs. Depending on just how offensive your excesses were, they can also prove remarkably effective the next morning. Fernet Branca, one of the most intense digestifs, is credited with fuelling much of the bar and restaurant trade the morning after a heavy night.

VERMOUTH Fortified wine is an umbrella definition that covers as many sins as successes. For every vintage port there is a Buckfast Tonic Wine; for every small-release en rama sherry, there is industrially produced cooking Marsala. Considerably less rock 'n' roll than its wormwood-based counterpart absinthe, vermouth has recently seen a boom in small, artisan producers and top-quality bottles.

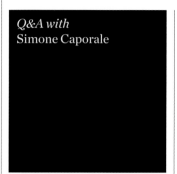

Q&A with
Simone Caporale

How did you get into the business? I was fascinated to see people's reactions when they received something that had been created by somebody else. Hospitality is all about delivering a great experience to the guest – it's more than just food and drink.

What is the key to making a great cocktail? It must be delicious, beautiful, look natural and genuine. It has to evoke a personal feeling, through either the garnish, or aroma or taste...a drink that can stimulate all five senses is a good drink, and it won't be forgotten by the consumer.

Who was your mentor/ bartending inspiration? I have had a few mentors in my career. I also take inspiration from anyone and anything...From guests to people I just see on the street. However, my main source of inspiration is Alex Kratena, Head Bartender at Artesian. He helped me discover a new way of thinking about the bar, what a bar should be and how to always look forward and push boundaries.

What is your favourite bar in the world, and why? Bar Boadas in Barcelona. For me, it represents a piece of living history where you can still see, and really feel, how bars have been an important element of our lives for many centuries. Obviously, times move on and it is important to look forward to continuously improve. However, it is important for me to appreciate and look at how our history can do this as well.

Traditionally a herbal/medicinal use for wine fortified with high-strength spirit, vermouth evolved in France and northern Italy and found its commercial feet in the early 20th century with established brands such as Cinzano, Martini and Noilly Prat. The basic styles are dry and sweet white (the former, an essential for a Martini) and sweet red (a key part of a Negroni and a Manhattan). It's the red that has dominated the cocktail world and that yields the greatest rewards in terms of different styles and producers. Instead of the excellent but commonplace Martini and Cinzano, bottles of vanilla-laced Antica Formula, warming Cocchi and bittersweet Punt e Mes are now the essential brands, alongside newer creations such as Casa Mariol from Spain and Sacred Spiced English vermouth.

ABSINTHE Over the last century, absinthe has been mythologized, demonized, faked, banned and legalized, to the extent that it is hard to tell if it has actually been enjoyably drunk at any point. It is unlikely that a modern bottle of absinthe would induce the visions, the artistic raptures and the hallucinations associated with the enjoyment of the drink by Toulouse-Lautrec and his fellow bohemians. The effects were often wildly exaggerated, and any feeling other than pure drunkenness was often down to the poor quality of production at the time. Absinthe has much in common with pastis, the clear aperitif that louches with the addition of water and whose bitter, herbal taste is nothing if not divisive. Both are derived from anise, a flavour found in so many native drinks of the Mediterranean, including raki and ouzo, although absinthe must base its botanicals around wormwood in order to qualify for the name.

One of the attributes that earned absinthe its dangerous reputation is its stratospheric ABV of up to 70 per cent. Hence it is more profitably, if cautiously, drunk well diluted with water. The addition of sugar is also optional, although the resulting drink should ideally retain a refreshing bitterness in order for the true flavours to be appreciated.

LIQUEURS Pity the liqueur. Left languishing at the back of an overcrowded shelf or cupboard, dusted off once a year, usually around Christmas, and drunk late at night when it either seems mistakenly like a good idea or is the only remaining alcoholic option. Truthfully, many liqueurs are best left in the cupboard, on the bar or, even better, in the shop, but there are some worth consideration. Cointreau or other triple sec liqueurs are useful for the odd pitcher of Margaritas – to liven up a basic meal of tacos, there is nothing like getting a few Margaritas under your belt. Baileys has made a pitch for respectability recently but remains distinctly in the 'guilty pleasure' category – by all means have a bottle stashed away, but proffering it enthusiastically to guests after a sophisticated dinner party may somewhat ruin the effect. Amaretto and curaçao lend their flavours to many worthy cocktails, crème de cassis will transform any bottle of ordinary sparkling wine into a decadent Kir Royale, and a nip of sloe gin is the best way to warm up a winter's day. The final essential? If you want a legal way to still be dancing like no one is watching at 4am then you'll need some Kahlúa for your espresso Martini.

Fog Cutter

This drink has been one of the pillars of Tiki cocktail culture since the Thirties and is considered to be the ancestor of the Long Island Iced Tea – not due to its ingredients, but because it is notoriously strong. Its name refers to the effect after drinking just one: you need something to 'clear the fog away from your eyes'! However, despite its generous alcohol content, the Fog Cutter has a marvellous flavour profile.

GLASSWARE
Highball

ICE
Cubes to shake, crushed ice to serve

GARNISH
The classic garnish would be slices of fruit (orange, lime or pineapple), but why not have some fun...seashells, a cocktail umbrella and even a wooden Brazilian swizzle.

SERVES 1

30ml (1fl oz) Jamaican rum
30ml (1fl oz) gin
30ml (1fl oz) Cognac
30ml (1fl oz) pineapple juice
50ml (1¾fl oz) orange juice
30ml (1fl oz) Disaronno
20ml (¾fl oz) lime juice
1 dash of Harvey's Bristol Cream sherry

Bartender's Tip
Many Tiki recipes call for orgeat syrup; however, this can easily be replaced with Disaronno liqueur, which has a bittersweet almond flavour.

Add all ingredients to a shaker with ice. Shake well, then strain into a chilled highball glass over crushed ice. Garnish with fruit slices...and whatever else takes your fancy!

Tuxedo

This cocktail takes its name from the bar where it was first created, The Tuxedo Club, which was established in 1886 in New York, USA. It is one of the many variations of the drink we know today as the Martini. The original recipe used two parts gin to one part dry sherry, and I consider it a great example of how a good gin Martini should have a strong wine-based element. Dry sherry, or dry vermouth, accentuates the gin's character within the cocktail, enhancing the taste of the drink, and also allowing us to appreciate the gin's flavour profile.

GLASSWARE
Sherry or wine

ICE
Cubes to stir, frozen river stones (*see* Bartender's Tip) to serve

GARNISH
Silver sugar balls (optional)

SERVES 1

60ml (2fl oz) Old Tom gin
40ml (1¼fl oz) dry vermouth
dash of maraschino liqueur (optional)
spray of absinthe

Add the gin, vermouth and maraschino, if using, to a mixing glass with ice and stir gently. Spray a chilled sherry or wine glass with absinthe, then add the frozen river stones. Strain the drink into the glass and add a few sugar balls if liked for decoration.

Bartender's Tip
Try using frozen 'stones' instead of ice cubes to serve the drink as they keep it cooler for longer without diluting it. Keep the stones in the freezer and use as required to enjoy your drink 'on the rocks'.

Godfather

The origin of the Godfather's name is uncertain; however, the liqueur brand Disaronno claims that the drink was the favourite cocktail of American actor Marlon Brando – most famous for his role as Don Corleone in Francis Ford Coppola's gangster epic, *The Godfather*. Brando apparently first requested the combination of Scotch whisky and Disaronno on 14 March 1972 at the New York Theatre Bar before the movie's world premiere. Subsequently, this unique blend was named after the movie.

GLASSWARE
Rocks

ICE
Large chunk

GARNISH
None

SERVES 1

50ml (1¾fl oz) Johnny Walker Black Label
25ml (¾fl oz) Disaronno

Bartender's Tip
For a slightly softer twist on the Godfather, swap the whisky for vodka and you will have yourself a Godmother. An offer you can't refuse?

Simply pour both ingredients into a chilled rocks glass containing a large chunk of ice and serve.

Turf Cocktail

A classic example of how Dutch gin and Italian vermouth go so well together in a glass. Different examples of the Turf Cocktail have been published in several cocktail books over the past century, but I think it works best as a simple aperitif. The drink is beautifully aromatic and floral due to the vermouth, while maintaining a rich and structured character thanks to the genever.

GLASSWARE
Coupe or Martini

ICE
Cubes to stir, none to serve

GARNISH
Lemon twist, olive-apple tower
(*see* Bartender's Tip)

SERVES 1

30ml (1fl oz) Martini Rosso
10ml (2 tsp) Martini Gran Lusso
40ml (1¼fl oz) genever
1 **dash** of absinthe
1 **dash** of Angostura bitters

Add all the ingredients to a shaker with ice. Stir, then strain into a chilled coupe or Martini glass. Garnish with a lemon twist and an olive-apple tower.

Bartender's Tip
As an additional garnish, a baby green apple and a Kalamata olive will provide an insane explosion of flavour in the mouth. It may sound bizarre, but the sweetness of the apple combined with the salty olive really works!

Champagne St Petersburg Cocktail

The Champagne Cocktail is one of the most classic and famous drinks. However, a common problem is that the hard, solid sugar cube takes a long time to dissolve. The consequence of this is that the cocktail on first sip isn't sweet enough, while the last sip can be too sweet. At the beginning of the 20th century in St Petersburg, bartenders served the Champagne Cocktail in a different way that resolved this problem (and is also a more attractive way of presenting the drink).

GLASSWARE
Flute

ICE
None

GARNISH
Orange twist

SERVES 1

2 tsp caster sugar
1 dash of Angostura bitters
20ml (¾fl oz) Cognac
100ml (3½fl oz) champagne

Place the flute into a freezer for 2 minutes or simply fill it with crushed ice and empty it after 30 seconds. Fill the glass with the sugar and gently rotate the flute in order to allow the sugar to coat the whole inner surface of the glass. Turn the flute upside down in order to remove any sugar that hasn't stuck to the glass. Add the Angostura bitters, pour in the Cognac and gently top up with the chilled champagne. Zest the orange twist to release the oils over the surface of the drink (*see* page 219) and discard the twist before serving.

Bartender's Tip
Pour the champagne into the glass very slowly so it won't fizz and the sugar will remain on the glass.

Champagne Punch

This fantastic rhyme first appeared in a great drinks book from 1869 called *Cooling Cups and Dainty Drinks*:
'Whene'er a bowl of punch we make,
 Four striking opposites we take.
 The strong, the small, the sharp, the sweet,
 Together mixed, most kindly meet.
 And when they happily unite,
 The bowl is fragrant with delight.'

GLASSWARE
Punch bowl, punch cups

ICE
Large chunks to serve

GARNISH
The more the merrier. Add lots of slices of fresh citrus fruits with a good handful of fresh berries and a sprinkle of edible rose petals to provide bursts of colour and an aromatic flavour

SERVES 10

750ml (1¼ pints) champagne
juice of **1** orange
1 small punnet raspberries
1 small punnet English strawberries, some sliced, some left whole
350ml (12fl oz) Ketel One vodka
150ml (¼ pint) pomegranate syrup
20ml (¾fl oz) rosewater
15 dashes of Peychaud's bitters
Juice of **3** lemons

Bartender's Tip
You can adjust the balance of citrus and sweet flavours by adding more or less lemon juice and syrup.

Pour all the ingredients into a punch bowl and stir together. Add the ice and garnish with fresh berries, citrus slices and rose petals.

Negroni

The Negroni is a true Italian cocktail symbol of the *aperitivo* hour. Now renowned worldwide, I actually believe that some credit for this cocktail's creation is owed to the UK (I will now be in trouble with my Italian colleagues!). After his trip to London in 1919, Count Negroni fell in love with London Dry gin so much he took some back to Florence with him. One day, he took his bottle of gin on his daily visit to Caffe Casoni and asked the barman, Fosco Scarselli, to prepare his usual Americano (Martini Rosso, Campari and soda water), but asked him to swap the soda water with gin, and the Negroni cocktail was born.

GLASSWARE
Rocks

ICE
Large sphere

GARNISH
Orange slice

SERVES 1

30ml (1fl oz) Tanqueray No. TEN gin
30ml (1fl oz) Martini Gran Lusso
30ml (1fl oz) Martini Bitter

Pour all the ingredients into a chilled rock glass containing a large ice sphere. Stir for a few seconds, then garnish with an orange slice.

Bartender's Tip
The classic twist on the Negroni is to swap the gin for bourbon to create a Boulevardier (*see* page 187).

Above & Beyond

This cocktail was created in 2013 at the The Langham hotel's Artesian Bar in London. This drink was inspired by Ron Zacapa, one of the finest rums, which is produced and carefully aged in the high mountains in Guatemala. The drink blends aged rum, a 30yo Pedro Ximénez sherry, Fernet and Tia Maria to provide a round and balanced drink. In addition, we decided to complement the drink with a multisensory garnish so the drink would touch all five senses. We developed a transparent 'pillow' that we inflate with the aroma of the Guatemalan rainforest to be presented on top of the drink.

GLASSWARE
Rocks

ICE
Cubes to stir, large sphere to serve

GARNISH
Guatemalan rainforest fragrance (or a lemon twist!)

SERVES 1

40ml (1¼fl oz) Ron Zacapa 23 rum
20ml (¾fl oz) Pedro Ximénez 30yo sherry
10ml (2 tsp) Tia Maria
5ml (1 tsp) Fernet

You will also need
Vaporizer
Inflatable pillow

Bartender's Tip
Serving this at home, a lemon twist garnish is fine!

Add all the ingredients to a mixing glass with ice. Stir, then strain into a chilled rocks glass containing a large ice sphere or chunk of ice.

For the authentic Artesian experience, serve this with a cloud of air from the Guatemalan rainforest (*see* above). To do this, use a vaporizer with aromas of wood, pine trees, eucalyptus, sandalwood and cedar tree to fill an inflatable pillow, and place over the drink. When the drink is served the 'cloud' is popped and the aroma escapes, surrounding the guest with a rainforest fragrance.

Leather-Aged Boulevardier

Over the past decade, bars around the world have been using the technique of ageing liquid in bottles or small barrels more and more frequently. It has become a popular trend in the bar industry and of particular interest to consumers. However, long before barrels were first made by humans, animal skin was used to carry and hold liquid. So we began to experiment with leather sacks to see how they would affect the flavour of our drinks. The result offered leathery, woody notes to the drink with subtle smokiness.

GLASSWARE
Rocks

ICE
Large sphere

GARNISH
Spanish chorizo slice, large caper berry

SERVES 1

30ml (1fl oz) Bulleit bourbon
30ml (1fl oz) Martini Bitter
30ml (1fl oz) Martini Rosso
15ml (½fl oz) Zucca Rabarbaro (rhubarb liqueur)

You will also need
1 large goatskin water sack

Bartender's Tip
Goatskin sacks can be obtained from leather shops, and are particularly easy to acquire on holiday.

Pour the ingredients into a large goatskin water sack. Leave the blend for no longer than 4–5 days. When ready to serve, pour the blend into a chilled rocks glass containing a large ice sphere. Garnish with a chorizo slice and a caper berry.

Rum Swizzle

A swizzle often refers to a stick that allows you to mix or stir liquid. From the Seventies, plastic stirrers became popular, but swizzle sticks were originally long natural wooden sticks taken from the 'swizzle tree', a short bush found in Central America and Hawaii. In terms of cocktails, a swizzle refers to a refreshing drink made with rum, lime juice, a spiced liqueur (such as a homemade falernum) and aromatic bitters like Angostura all mixed together over crushed ice with a traditional swizzle stick.

GLASSWARE
Highball

ICE
Crushed ice to mix, and to serve

GARNISH
Use a wooden swizzle stick as a garnish in addition to a mint sprig, a lime wedge, and a float of Angostura bitters...or be as playful as you wish (I like to serve mine with an alligator's head and Barbie Doll sombrero!)

SERVES 1

50ml (1¾fl oz) Ron Zacapa 23 rum
30ml (1fl oz) falernum liqueur
20ml (¾fl oz) lime juice
5ml (1 tsp) Isolabella sambuca
3 shiso leaves

Bartender's Tip
You can make your own falernum liqueur, but you may find it easier to buy a bottle of John D Taylor's Velvet Falernum liqueur.

Add all the ingredients to a chilled highball glass. Add crushed ice and use a wooden swizzle stick to 'swizzle-it' for 10 seconds. Top up with more crushed ice, then garnish as you please...

Aqui Estoy

Tequila is a fantastic spirit – as versatile as vodka, as tasty as gin and as complex as whisky. It makes a wide variety of extraordinary cocktails and offers an array of tasting notes, which sadly go unnoticed when it is just shot at parties. I also believe that many people haven't experienced a good-quality tequila. Don Julio is widely revered as the best – it uses hand-selected ripened blue agave and is produced using artisanal methods. It has a smooth character and is a great example of fine tequila. This is a refreshing cocktail that showcases the flavours of tequila with the addition of Falernum.

GLASSWARE
We serve it in a skull wearing a Mexican hat, with rice flowers in the eyeballs. If you don't have a skull to hand, a highball glass is fine!

ICE
Crushed ice to serve

GARNISH
Lime slice, stick of Chinese bark... with smoke of a Mexican market (*see* method)!

SERVES 1

50ml (1¾fl oz) Don Julio tequila
20ml (¾fl oz) lime juice
30ml Falernum syrup
dash of rose water

Bartender's Tip
If you have one, place a small straw hat (preferably a Mexican sombrero) on top of the drink, to keep the smoke inside until you serve the drink.

Add all the ingredients to a chilled highball glass (or skull) with crushed ice. Add a lime slice and a stick of Chinese bark. Burn the bark with a lighter or cook's blowtorch to create an aromatic smoke, then serve.

Langham Martini

The plan was to create the ultimate gin Martini and in 2012 I think we achieved it. The Langham Martini is prepared with Tanqueray No. TEN gin, the finest crystal-clear ice and a choice of five hand-crafted dry vermouths, each of them with subtle hints of flavours inspired by iconic destinations from around the world. At the bar, we serve it in a bespoke silver vessel that provides an interactive ritual for the guest and ensures the drink is kept at the perfect temperature for longer. We perfume the drink with aromatic citrus oils and serve with a side of olives macerated with the Tanqueray No. TEN botanicals.

GLASSWARE
Silver Martini

ICE
Top-quality ice to stir, none to serve

GARNISH
Lemon twist (discarded), Nocellara del Belice olives

SERVES 1

30ml (1fl oz) Martini Extra Dry vermouth
70ml (2¼fl oz) Tanqueray No. TEN gin
few drops of elderflower cordial (optional)

Add the vermouth and gin to a mixing glass with ice. To make 'bespoke vermouth' as we do at Artesian, add a few drops of elderflower cordial to your vermouth before adding the gin, if liked. Stir, then strain into a chilled Martini glass. Zest the lemon twist to release the oils over the surface of the drink (*see* page 219), then discard the twist. Serve with a dish of Nocellara del Belice olives.

Bartender's Tip
When you make a Martini, bear in mind that ice is not just a tool to chill and dilute the drink – it should also be considered as an ingredient. Why? Good-quality ice makes a good-quality drink – use filtered water if possible.

Pink Bamboo

This is a twist on the classic Bamboo cocktail, originally made with dry sherry and dry vermouth. Not surprisingly, the drink was quite dry and only really appreciated by those who enjoyed the crisp notes that fortified wine such as dry sherry can deliver. I decided to swap the sherry with Genmai sake; 'Genmai' means 'aged' and so the sake provides a deliciously nutty, fruity taste. Instead of dry vermouth, I use a Rosato vermouth, pink in colour with a nutmeg and raspberry flavour profile. In addition, adding a few drops of maraschino liqueur helps to blend the two liquids together.

Add all the ingredients to a shaker with ice. Stir, then strain into a sake cup or sea urchin shell. Garnish with oyster leaves and a pearl onion (and perhaps a tasty grasshopper).

GLASSWARE
Sake dry clay cup or a sea urchin shell

ICE
Cubes to stir, none to serve

GARNISH
Oyster leaves, pearl onions. If using grasshoppers, pan-fry with garlic and lime

SERVES 1

50ml (1¾fl oz) Akashi-Tai Genmai aged sake (infused with grasshopper)
50ml (1¾fl oz) Martini Rosato
dash of Mandarin bitters
few drops of Maraschino liqueur

Bartender's Tip
As a savoury drink this makes a great aperitif. It is an interesting alternative to more traditional savoury cocktails such as the Bloody Mary.

Forever Young

The Langham in London was Europe's first grand hotel and has a fascinating history. Oscar Wilde was a regular guest and it is believed that he wrote *The Picture of Dorian Gray* while at the hotel. We used this as the inspiration for the Forever Young cocktail. In our research for creating garnishes that entice all of the senses, we looked at how we could include a mirror with our drink (such a powerful visual element for humans – we cannot help but look at our reflection). This resulted in us creating a mirrored serve, where the drinks glass sits behind the mirror so guests see their reflection as they drink.

GLASSWARE
Short silver glass

ICE
Cubes to shake, none to serve

GARNISH
Small pocket mirror (the garnish is the picture of you, reflected in the mirror)

SERVES 1

50ml (1¾fl oz) Ketel One vodka
20ml (¾fl oz) eucalyptus liqueur
20ml (¾fl oz) Martini Extra Dry
15ml (½fl oz) lemon juice
5ml (1 tsp) maraschino liqueur
Splash of soda water

Add all ingredients except the soda water to a shaker with ice. Shake, then add a splash of soda. Strain into a glass and serve with a mirror garnish.

Bartender's Tip
If you don't have a silver glass, a rocks glass will work (it just won't be as much fun!).

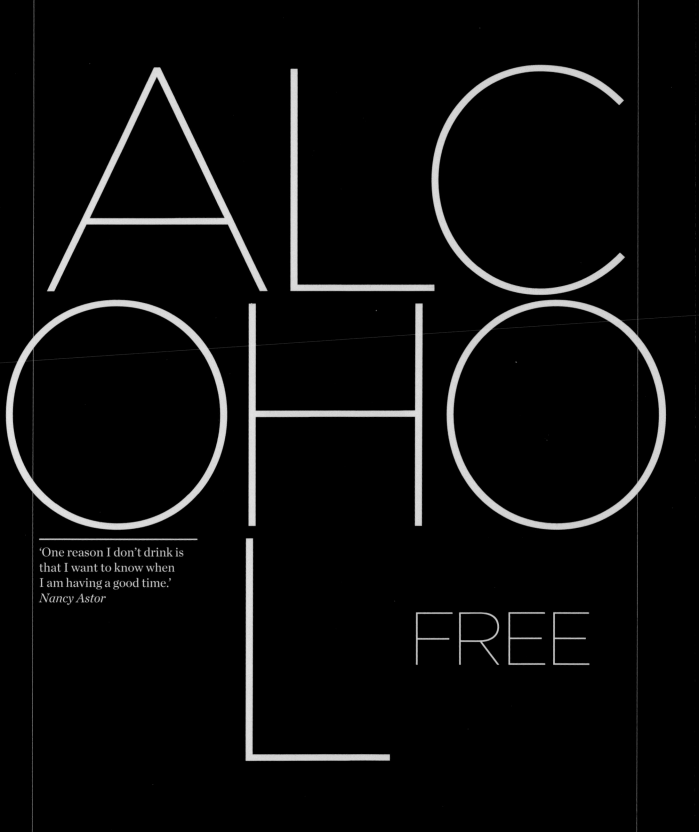

ALCOHOL FREE

'One reason I don't drink is that I want to know when I am having a good time.'
Nancy Astor

Recipes by Ryan Chetiyawardana

White Lyan, London

Alcohol-free
by Paul Henderson

Alcohol-free cocktails, it would be fair to say, have something of a reputation. Depending on your point of view, it could be a reputation for being boring, a reputation for being holier-than-thou, or a reputation for being one decent ingredient short of a proper drink. However, if they are made correctly and shown the same thought and consideration as traditional alcoholic creations, they can offer all the delicious and refreshing flavours of a cocktail with none of those pesky side effects.

Before you can enjoy a decent virgin cocktail, it is important to get a few misconceptions out of the way. First, there is the issue over who drinks them. In no particular order, the usual suspects are:
• Designated drivers. Expanding on the old adage that 'if you won't take the bus, don't make a fuss', the man or woman who will start and end the night with a steering wheel in front of them shouldn't spend the evening with an alcoholic drink in front of them either.
• Pregnant women. Aside from a formal announcement and a baby shower, nothing tells your friends that you have a bun in the oven quicker than ordering a mocktail in a bar.
• Children. To be fair, they have a pretty good excuse.
But if this list serves no other purpose, it at least confirms that what you think you know about the typical alcohol-free cocktail consumer is wrong. In the 21st century, more and more people are choosing to abstain from 'the demon drink' than ever before. It could be for health reasons, to reduce their alcohol intake, or even down to problems from drinking, but whatever the cause of their sobriety, non-drinkers can now enjoy 'soft' options hand-crafted by a new generation of talented mixologists who regard creating virgin cocktails as just as much of a challenge as finding new ways to celebrate spirits.

Of course, coming up with alcohol-free drinks has a history every bit as interesting and intriguing as the legendary fermented libations you have already heard about. From a historical perspective, you can go back almost as far as you like. The Indians, Egyptians and Aztecs all mixed different liquids for taste and flavour (and in the case of Montezuma and his hot chocolate, as an aphrodisiac). By the Middle Ages, drinks such as sage water, non-fermented apple ciders and chicory water (as mentioned in Cervantes' Don Quixote) were enjoyed without fear of a hangover. And then came the era of Prohibition in the US, when creating drinks mimicking the hard cocktails that were then illegal had its moment in the sun (admittedly, more out of necessity than desire), with Bertha E L Stockbridge's *What To Drink: The Blue Book of Beverages – Recipes and Directions for Making and Serving Non-Alcoholic Drinks for All Occasions* going some way to easing Americans into 20th-century temperance.

As a precursor to the maxim that bartenders live by to this day, Bertha wrote, 'The hostess of today will be called upon to serve drinks in her home more than formerly, I imagine, and it would be well to go back to the habits and customs of our grandmothers and be prepared to serve a refreshing drink in an attractive manner at a moment's notice.'

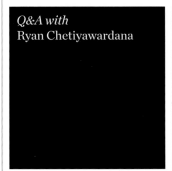

While the ethos was right, the desire (and demand) for alcohol far outweighed Mrs Stockbridge's ambitious abstemiousness. And yet the flavoured syrups and herb-scented sodas (as demonstrated in her Georgia Mint Julep and Strawberry-Lemon Froth) paved the way for the exciting experimentation currently being employed by bartenders keen to expand their repertoires.

Today, at some of the most celebrated bars, you will find a 'mocktail' selection that bears comparison with any classic cocktail you care to mention. In London, for example, at the Connaught Bar you can try a Sundance (orange and peach juice, with vanilla sugar, grenadine and soda), Claridge's Bar serves a Cuban Cooler (as good as a Mojito, minus the rum) and the Artesian Bar (aka the Best Bar in the World) offers a G&Tea that dispenses with gin but delivers a selection of botanicals in a homemade soda. *The Sunday Times*'s famously teetotal restaurant critic A A Gill wrote that Mark Hix's Bar in London's Soho served him 'the best non-alcoholic cocktail I've ever had, based on green tea and lime'.

And now there are even bars purely for the teetotaller. In the UK, The Brink in Liverpool became the first UK dry bar when it opened in 2011 and has seen its popularity rise and profits increase significantly, counting HRH the Duchess of Cambridge as its Patron. The current bar manager, Jacquie Johnston-Lynch, who was named the 2013 Social Entrepreneur of the Year for her efforts, is advising other dry bars looking to set up around the country. According to Johnston-Lynch's research, in a survey of Londoners under the age of 30, three-quarters of them said they would visit an alcohol-free bar. This seems borne out by Catherine Salway who, after a series of successful pop-ups, founded Redemption, a small chain of 'alcohol-free gastrobars' in London that are as atmospheric as any speakeasy you'll find buried in a basement with a secret entrance. 'I came up with the idea of a really cool alcohol-free bar concept about two years ago, and when I first started sharing the idea with friends and family they thought I was mad,' says Salway. 'By the time I'd launched in July 2013 I felt I was on the cusp of the zeitgeist, and now everyone's talking about it!'

Salway describes the Redemption clientele as 'typically younger (in the 25–34 age bracket), educated, hip, unafraid to try new things, and caring about how they look'. At the moment, she says, more women than men are visiting (the split is 60/40), but the global trend for people looking for ways to improve their health is universal and growing in popularity all the time. Living a clean lifestyle is also linking in to socializing, making a dry bar the perfect meeting point. It would not work, however, if the drinks didn't match the mood.

'We go for really fresh organic fruit and vegetables with a lot of herbs and spices,' Salway explains. 'Our most popular drinks are the Coco-rita (coconut water, fresh lime, agave syrup and Himalayan rock salt) and the Apple Mock-jito (muddled mint, lime and apple juice topped with sparkling water). They taste as sophisticated as real cocktails, but they are actually really good for you.'

Well...what are you waiting for?

Virgin Southside

The original gin-based Southside cocktail is one of those drinks with hotly debated origins. Whether it came from Prohibition-era Chicago, New York's legendary speakeasy the 21 Club, or the Southside Sportsmen's Club in Long Island is up for debate – but there is no debate about the light and refreshing quality of this cocktail even with the gin removed. This twist delivers a floral flavour with a green bite from the pressed apple and mint leaves. The ginger ale adds a nice touch of spice and effervescence.

GLASSWARE
Highball or sling

ICE
Crushed or cracked to stir and to serve

GARNISH
Mint sprig

SERVES 1

50ml (1¾fl oz) pressed apple juice
12 mint leaves
10ml (2 tsp) elderflower cordial
Ginger ale, to top up

Build apple, mint and cordial in a sling or highball glass over crushed or cracked ice and stir. Add more ice, then top up with ginger ale. Garnish with a mint sprig.

Bartender's Tip
Use a high-quality ginger ale such as Fever-Tree. You want a nice candied spiciness from the ginger, rather than something too sweet.

Bora Bora Brew

Mocktails can sometimes be accused of lacking that alcoholic kick that comes from a well-constructed drink, but not with the Bora Bora Brew. As you would expect, it is heavily flavoured with the tropical notes of pineapple and ginger – it is named after an island in French Polynesia, after all – but that is balanced out by a good dose of spice from the bitters and the tart sweetness of the grenadine.

GLASSWARE
Highball or sling

ICE
Cubes to shake and to serve

GARNISH
Lemon wedge or slice, raspberries

SERVES 1

50ml (1¾fl oz) pineapple juice
10ml (2 tsp) proper grenadine
3 dashes of Angostura bitters
Ginger ale, to top up

Add all the ingredients except the ginger ale to a shaker with ice. Shake, then strain into a sling or highball glass over cubed ice and top up with ginger ale. Garnish with a lemon wedge or slice and raspberries.

Bartender's Tip
There are a few artisan grenadine producers now. Try Blossoms grenadine, which has the earthy depth of true pomegranates, rather than a sickly sweet red syrup.

Bajan Cooler

Coolers always make the best summer drinks because they are long, light and refreshing. This one is inspired by the Caribbean island of Barbados, and what it lacks in rum, it makes up for with a crisp, thirst-quenching taste. The spice from the ginger beer and the basil cuts through the apple and honey, leaving a complex serve that evolves as it dilutes.

Add all the ingredients except the ginger beer to a shaker with ice and stir until the honey has dissolved. Shake, then double strain (*see* page 219) into a chilled highball glass over ice and top up with ginger beer. Garnish with basil leaves and a sprig of mint.

GLASSWARE
Highball or sling

ICE
Cubes to shake and to serve

GARNISH
Basil leaves, mint sprig

SERVES 1

5ml (1 tsp) clear honey
50ml (1¾fl oz) pressed apple juice
20ml (¾fl oz) fresh lime juice
5 basil leaves
Ginger beer, to top up

Bartender's Tip
Stir the honey with the juices first. Make sure it has all dissolved before you shake it.

Vanilla Chocolate

If you were to cross a Virgin Vanilla Chocolate Martini with a frothy shake, you would probably come up with this, which is sweet but certainly not sickly. What you end up with is a simple homemade soda with the creamy and decadent indulgence of vanilla and chocolate. Make sure you use cacoa nibs, which have a milder flavour and are less bitter than chocolate.

GLASSWARE
Highball or sling

ICE
None to prepare, cubes to serve

GARNISH
Lemon slice

SERVES 1

30ml (1fl oz) vanilla and cacoa-nib syrup (*see* below)
Soda water, to top up

For the vanilla and cacoa-nib syrup
(Makes 500ml/18fl oz)
500g (1lb) demerara sugar
400ml (14fl oz) water
20g (¾oz) cacoa nibs
1 split vanilla pod

Bartender's Tip
If you prefer something a little less candied, you can add a pinch of salt to the drink at the end, which tones down the sweetness.

First make the syrup. Put all the syrup ingredients in a saucepan and heat until the sugar has dissolved. Remove from the heat and leave to infuse and cool. Strain, then bottle in a sterilized container and refrigerate until ready to use.

To make the cocktail, pour the vanilla and cacao-nib syrup into a chilled highball glass over ice and top up with soda water. Garnish with a lemon slice.

Pineapple Cardamom Brew

I know what you are probably thinking, but please don't be off put by the cardamom – or by the quantity of it – that appears in this recipe. As a spice, cardamom has a powerful flavour, hence its regular appearance in Indian cooking, but rather than overpowering this drink as you might expect, its smoky richness offsets the natural sweetness of the pineapple. The ginger beer provides an effervescent finish and a spicy nod in the right direction.

GLASSWARE
Highball or sling

ICE
None to prepare, cubes to serve

GARNISH
Lemon slice, mint sprig

SERVES 1

30ml (1fl oz) pineapple cardamom syrup (*see* below)
Ginger beer, to top up

For the pineapple cardamom syrup
(Makes 500ml/18fl oz)
500ml (18 fl oz) pineapple juice
200g (7oz) caster sugar
6 cardamom pods

Bartender's Tip
Green cardamom pods give a wonderful warm spiciness, but you could substitute the larger, black pods, which have more of a citrussy, eucalyptus lead.

First make the syrup. Put all the syrup ingredients in a saucepan and heat until the sugar has dissolved. Remove from the heat and leave to infuse and cool. Strain, then bottle in a sterilized container and refrigerate until ready to use.

To make the cocktail, pour the pineapple cardamom syrup into a chilled highball glass over ice and top up with ginger beer. Garnish with a lemon slice and a mint sprig.

Smoked Coconut

Highly popular for a long time in Brazil, India and the Caribbean, and increasingly so elsewhere, coconut water is natural, high in antioxidants and minerals, especially potassium, low in calories and great for hydration. To give it a little flavour makeover, try this mocktail. The subtle smoked flavour, created using a smoke gun, complements the tropical notes of the coconut, creating an unusual but moreish drink.

GLASSWARE
Highball or sling

ICE
None to prepare, cubes to serve

GARNISH
Fresh banana slices

SERVES 1

30ml (1fl oz) smoked sweetened coconut water
Soda water, to top up

For the smoked sweetened coconut water
(Makes 500ml/18fl oz)
500ml (18fl oz) coconut water
300g (10oz) caster sugar

You will also need
Smoke gun

Bartender's Tip
Smoke guns are a great way of adding in a dry smoky edge. You can also then begin to experiment with different wood, and even herb, smoke flavours.

First make the smoked sweetened coconut water. Put the coconut water and sugar in a Kilner jar, then fill with smoke using a smoke gun. Seal the jar and shake. Fill the jar with more smoke and shake again until all the sugar has dissolved.

To make the cocktail, pour the smoked sweetened coconut water into a chilled highball glass over ice and top up with soda water. Garnish with banana slices.

Cherry Ginger Cooler

Maraschino cherries may be familiar in a cocktail, but cherry juice is probably far less so. The obvious pairing with cherry juice is chocolate, plum or apricot, but for this adult cooler we are mixing things up. The sweetness from the sugar balances the tartness of the cherries, the fresh ginger provides a spicy hit, and the soda water gives a fizzy and refreshing lightness. A real summer special.

GLASSWARE
Highball or sling

ICE
None to prepare, cubes to serve

GARNISH
Berries, mint sprig

First make the syrup. Put the syrup ingredients in a saucepan and heat until the sugar has dissolved. Remove from the heat and leave to infuse and cool. Strain, then bottle in a sterilized container and refrigerate until ready to use.

To make the cocktail, pour the cherry and ginger syrup into a chilled highball glass over ice and top up with soda water. Garnish with berries and a mint sprig.

SERVES 1

30ml (1fl oz) cherry and ginger syrup (*see* below)
Soda water, to top up

For the cherry and ginger syrup (Makes 500ml/18fl oz)
500ml (18fl oz) cherry juice
100g (3½oz) white sugar
Thumb-sized piece of fresh ginger

Bartender's Tip
If you want a more pronounced ginger note, grate the ginger, or add fresh ginger juice while the syrup is cooling.

Lemonade

Anyone can make lemonade, right? Yes, of course they can...but not everyone can make it well. Leagues away from the shop-bought clear stuff, this simple recipe is surprisingly complex and wonderfully refreshing. The key is probably the little pinch of salt, which gives the citrus taste a boost and dials down the tartness – just don't add too much!

GLASSWARE
Highball or sling

ICE
Cubes to shake and to serve

GARNISH
Lemon slice

SERVES 1

50ml (1¾fl oz) freshly pressed lemon juice
15ml (½fl oz) sugar syrup
1 pinch of salt
Soda water, to top up

Bartender's Tip
Squeeze your lemon juice to order to make sure it has the right zestiness. Use a hand squeezer – or 'Mexican elbow' – to get all the oils from the skin, too.

Add all the ingredients except the soda water to a shaker with ice. Shake, then strain into a chilled sling glass with ice and top up with soda water. Garnish with a lemon slice.

Lavender Fizz

Strictly speaking, this is not an alcohol-free cocktail because of the inclusion of bitters, but it is such a negligible amount that we think you will get away with it (or you could leave it out if you wish). And anyway, the real story of this cocktail is the lavender. Aromatic and soothing, the light botanical flavour of the drink is floral, but it is given a sophisticated twist by the citrus (and the bitters, if you are living dangerously!).

GLASSWARE
Highball or sling

ICE
Cubes to shake and to serve

GARNISH
Orange slice, lavender sprig

SERVES 1

30ml (1fl oz) fresh lemon juice
30ml (1fl oz) orange juice
20ml (¾fl oz) lavender syrup
2 dashes of orange bitters
Soda water, to top up

Add all the ingredients except the soda water to a shaker with ice. Shake, then strain into a sling glass with ice and top up with soda water. Garnish with an orange slice and a lavender sprig.

Bartender's Tip
Lavender syrups can be bought, but when the flowers are in season it is better simply to infuse the heads in a warm sugar syrup (*see* page 220).

'Shandy'

Originally known as shandygaff in England and supposedly described by Charles Dickens as 'an alliance between beer and pop', this beverage is the quintessential British summer drink. Traditionally, it is a simple mix of beer and lemonade, but this alcohol-free twist delivers a similar balance of malt and citrus. Zesty and bright, it also has a nutty undertone that adds complexity and a yeasty hit to replace the missing beer.

GLASSWARE
Highball or sling

ICE
Cubes to shake and to serve

GARNISH
Orange slice

Add all the ingredients except the soda water to a shaker with ice. Shake, then strain into a sling glass with ice and top up with soda water. Garnish with an orange slice.

SERVES 1

20ml (¾fl oz) freshly squeezed lemon juice
20ml (¾fl oz) freshly squeezed orange juice
20ml (¾fl oz) freshly squeezed grapefruit juice
20ml (¾fl oz) malt extract syrup
Soda water, to top up

Bartender's Tip
Malt extract is best bought from a brew shop or online where you can find this nutty, caramel-style syrup. I recommend Thomas Coopers malt extract.

Hot 'Iced' Tea

This is a fun and playful cocktail to add to your alcohol-free repertoire. In essence, it is a deconstructed twist on the classic American iced tea – only sweetened with honey instead of sugar. Serve it in a teacup for a little English authenticity, and remember to add the component parts one at a time to keep things theatrical. The interesting quality about this drink is that the flavour notes change as it cools, so you can enjoy it hot or cold.

GLASSWARE
Teacup or mug

ICE
Tea cube (*see* method)

GARNISH
Mint sprig

SERVES 1

30ml (1fl oz) lemon juice
15ml (1 tbsp) clear honey

For the tea cubes
20g (¾oz) Rare Tea Company Earl Grey tea leaves
Grated zest of **2** lemons, **1** orange and **1** grapefruit
500ml (18fl oz) boiling water

Bartender's Tip
Keep a tray of tea cubes in the freezer – they can be used in a variety of hot and cold cocktails to slowly release tea flavour and tannins.

First make the tea cubes. Put the tea leaves and citrus zest in a heatproof bowl, then pour over the boiling water. Leave to steep for 10 minutes, then strain into ice cube moulds and freeze.

To make the cocktail, add the lemon juice and honey to a teacup and top up with hot water. Stir, then add a tea cube. Garnish with a mint sprig.

Spiced Honey Lemon

This is not so much a cocktail as a full-flavoured tonic. The ingredients in the Spiced Honey Lemon deliver a well-being explosion that will have you feeling great just by sniffing it. The lemon grass has antioxidant qualities, the ginger helps digestion, the black peppercorns have antibacterial properties, the cardamom acts as a diuretic, the cloves are natural painkillers and the honey contains flavonoids that are thought to reduce the risk of getting some cancers. This is literally a little cup of good health and great flavour, offering the comforting bliss of a hot toddy, without the jolting whack of booze.

GLASSWARE
Teacup

ICE
None

GARNISH
Lemon twist

SERVES 1

500ml (18fl oz) water
1 sliced lemon grass stalk
5 black peppercorns
2 cardamom pods
2 cloves
slice of fresh root ginger
10ml (2 tsp) clear honey

Pour the water into a saucepan and add the sliced lemon grass, peppercorns, cardamom pods, cloves and ginger. Bring to the boil, then strain into a teacup. Stir in the honey and garnish with a lemon twist.

Bartender's Tip
Experiment with different accent spices – start by substituting one at a time to work out your favourite combination.

Aztec Hot Chocolate

It probably would not come as a surprise to find this cocktail in almost any of the other chapters in this book. You could add rum, brandy, tequila or even whisky if you were so inclined – but why bother when the alcohol-free version is so delicious, warming and indulgent on its own? With plenty of aromatic and exciting spices to offset the richness of the chocolate, this is decadent and extravagant in the extreme.

GLASSWARE
Mug

ICE
None

GARNISH
Cinnamon sticks

SERVES 1

50g (2oz) good-quality dark chocolate
1 pinch of sea salt
10ml (2 tsp) granulated sugar
50ml (1¾fl oz) cream
200ml (7fl oz) full-fat milk
1 pinch of chilli powder
1 pinch of ground cinnamon
1 pinch of ground allspice
1 pinch of grated nutmeg

Bartender's Tip
Mild chilli powder gives a hint of fruity, background spice to the chocolate. If you are brave enough, increase the amount to give a bolder contrast.

In a bain-marie, melt the dark chocolate over low heat. Once it has formed a liquid, whisk in the salt, sugar, cream and milk. When it has all been incorporated and the sugar has dissolved, add the chilli powder, cinnamon, allspice and nutmeg. Pour into a mug and garnish with cinnamon sticks.

Mulled Apple

Definitely one for autumn and winter, this cocktail is not diminished by substituting apple for cider. In fact, it is so delicious and complex that you might wonder why you bothered with fermented apples in the first place. Spicy and with enough sugar to offset the tartness of the apples, it is the perfect cocktail to help you brave the outdoors. Or serve it next to a roaring fire – especially if you take the time to offer it to your guests in a hollowed-out apple.

GLASSWARE
4 hollowed-out apples
(*see* Bartender's Tip)

ICE
None

GARNISH
Lemon twists, grated nutmeg

SERVES 4

500ml (18fl oz) pressed apple
  juice
1 cinnamon stick
15ml (1 tbsp) cider vinegar
50g (2oz) demerara sugar
2 cloves
1 vanilla pod, split

Put all the ingredients in a saucepan and bring to the boil. Remove from the heat and leave to infuse. Strain into hollowed-out apples and garnish each with a lemon twist and grated nutmeg to taste.

Bartender's Tip
Use a corer and an old-style lemon squeezer to remove the flesh of the apples and form the hollowed-out cups in which to serve the drink.

Café de Olla

The origins of this cocktail can be found in the traditional Mexican coffee, known as Café de Olla, served in earthenware pots, with cinnamon and unrefined cane sugar (*piloncillo*). To add a twist on the traditional spiced coffee, this version uses Sweetshop espresso – a really fruity, sweet and acidic blend that is counterbalanced by aniseed.

GLASSWARE
Mug

ICE
None

GARNISH
None

SERVES 2

500ml (18 fl oz) water
5ml (1 tsp) molasses
80g (3oz) demerara sugar
1 cinnamon stick
5ml (1 tsp) aniseed
20g (¾oz) Square Mile
  Sweetshop espresso coffee

Bartender's Tip
This can also be made as a coffee cold-drip, or cold brew, giving a fruitier take on the cocktail.

Put all the ingredients except the coffee in a saucepan and bring to the boil. Remove from the heat and add the coffee. Leave to infuse for 5 minutes, then strain thorough a coffee filter into mugs and serve.

Glassware, Techniques & Kit

GLASSWARE

This is not quite a definitive list of every vessel featured in *GQ Drinks* (as you will see, most of our bartenders use their own bespoke beakers and we would not feel comfortable recommending just any old hollowed-out skull), but if you have the glassware featured here you won't go too far wrong. As a rough guide, when it comes to glassware four is the magic number: if you have a coupe, a highball, a flute and a rocks glass, you can get away with 90 per cent of the cocktails featured in *GQ Drinks*.

Note: for cold cocktails, all glassware should be chilled in the freezer before serving.

Brandy balloon (1)
Unlike other glasses, the brandy balloon (or snifter) is designed to be cradled in your hand, thereby warming the cocktail and boosting the aromas. *Classically used for:* Stinger

Collins (2)
A tall glass designed to hold plenty of ice and liquid, this is ideally suited to Tiki-style fruit cocktails or long drinks with mixers. *Classically used for:* El Diablo and Tom Collins

Coupe/coupette (3)
The classic champagne bowl has enjoyed a resurgence in popularity over the last decade (especially given everyone's favourite myth, that its design was modelled on Marie Antoinette's left breast). *Classically used for:* Sover au Champagne and Vodka Espresso

Flute (4)
The tall, narrow champagne flute is designed so that the surface area of the drink is reduced, thereby retaining its carbonation for longer. *Classically used for:* Champagne Cocktail and Bellini

Highball/sling (5)
Similar to a Collins glass (but slightly narrower), this straight-sided glass is for long drinks served with either cubes or crushed ice. *Classically used for:* Gin Fizz and Fog Cutter

Hurricane (6)
The legendary Hurricane cocktail has its very own glass, which has become synonymous with tropical Tiki drinks (and by extension, big umbrellas). *Classically used for:* Hurricane and The Painkiller

Margarita (7)
Based on the champagne coupe but often a little deeper, the Margarita is a popular cocktail glass for drinks served straight up. *Classically used for:* Margarita and Daiquiri

Martini/cocktail (8)
With its iconic triangular silhouette, this glass is designed for small drinks served without ice. To keep your drink cold, hold it by the stem. *Classically used for:* Martini and Manhattan

Rocks/lowball (9)
The shorter, fatter cousin of the highball glass, the rocks glass is designed so that short, strong drinks can be served with ice (to soften the alcohol burn). *Classically used for:* Old Fashioned and Manhattan

Sherry (10)
Not just for the maiden aunt's favourite tipple at Christmas, the sherry glass has been utilized by bartenders because it is smaller than a wine glass and perfect for aperitifs. *Classically used for:* The Hanky-Panky and Copita

Shot (11)
This small glass is designed specifically for a single measure of spirit. *Classically used for:* whisky and vodka (neat)

Teacup (12)
A fun and increasingly common vessel used by mixologists for both hot and cold cocktails, this is especially popular for tea-infused drinks. *Classically used for:* Gin Tea Punch

Wine (13)
Wine glasses come in a variety of shapes and sizes, but an average one holds more liquid than a champagne flute. Again, it should be held by the stem to keep the cocktail cold. *Classically used for:* Cobblers

All glassware featured, courtesy of John Lewis, www.johnlewis.com

COCKTAIL KIT

From shakers and stirrers to strainers and sieves, modern mixologists have a veritable cocktail compendium at their disposal. You won't need anywhere near as much equipment as they use (unless you plan on following the Modernist approach to cocktail-making, in which case you might need a chemistry set, too) but there are a few essentials you cannot get by without.

Cocktail shaker (14)
Although they are available in many different shapes and sizes, in essence shakers come in two varieties – the traditional standard shaker and the Boston two-piece shaker. The standard shaker is the best for beginners and is made up of three parts: a flat-bottomed lower can, an upper top with a pouring funnel and strainer, and a cap. The Boston shaker is made up of a large cone (usually made of steel) and a glass that is slightly smaller and fits inside. Boston shakers tend to be larger than the standard shaker and are aimed at budding bartenders with more skill and expertise.

Ice bucket and ice tongs (15)
Bartenders take their ice very seriously. For instance, most recommend using filtered water to remove any impurities. The type of ice you use depends on the drink being made, but whether it be cubes, crushed ice or blocks, it helps to have an ice bucket to hand to keep it in. Before transferring the ice to it, chill the bucket in the freezer along with your ice tongs, and you'll keep your frozen H_2O in perfect condition.

Stirrer (16)
No, it's not just a big spoon (it's more like a really long spoon). For cocktails that rely on stirring (or swizzling) rather than shaking, a decent stirrer is essential. Ideally made of stainless steel, it should be slender and comfortable to hold. You can chill your stirrer in the freezer before using it, if you like.

10 · 11 · 12 · 13 · 14 · 15

Mixing glass (17)
For cocktails that are to be stirred, and especially when muddling is employed, a mixing glass is really useful. It should be strong and sturdy (often the glass half of a Boston shaker will suffice), but never used for serving a cocktail.

Strainer (18)
The Hawthorn strainer is an essential tool for guaranteeing a smooth, clear cocktail. After all, there is nothing worse than a cocktail contaminated with unwanted shards of ice or lumps of fruit. Hold the strainer over your mixing glass, and the spring around the outer ridge should stop any unwanted extras.

Jigger (19)
A cocktail without the right measure of ingredients is not a cocktail. Well, it is...but it probably won't taste as good as it should. Therefore, a cocktail jigger is vital for guaranteeing both quantity and, by extension, quality. The most common jigger is double-ended: one end holds 20 or 25ml (¾fl oz), the other 40 or 50ml (1¼ or 1¾fl oz). Alternatively, you can use chef's measuring spoons.

Bottle opener (20)
It might seem blindingly obvious, but a good bottle opener is a must – even if you only use it for opening a bottle of wine or a beer when you are all cocktailed out!

Muddler
A mixologist's muddler is really just a blunt, or slightly jagged, pestle for mashing fruit, herbs, sugar and spices to release their juice, oils and aromas – think of your mixing glass or shaker as the mortar.

You will also need
A juicer (21), a decent knife and a chopping board, an ice scoop, a peeler, a grater and a fine tea strainer (22, *see* Straining).

For decoration
You might like to use straws, umbrellas and swizzle sticks.

To take your cocktails to the next level
Invest in a soda siphon, an atomizer and a blender.

Cocktail kit courtesy of Alessi, www.alessi.com

TECHNIQUES

Throughout *GQ Drinks* you will find tips and techniques for using specific individual ingredients, but there are some universal cocktail-making methods that are essential.

Shaking
Fill a cocktail shaker with cubed ice to approximately two-thirds full, and add your ingredients. Make sure the lid is secure, then shake rhythmically using two hands for roughly 10–15 seconds. This should be enough to chill a strong drink to around -3°C (26.6°F) – at which temperature a frosty condensation should form on the outside of the shaker – and dilute it a little. Remember to shake vigorously and keep a firm grip.

Dry shaking
For drinks containing egg (usually egg white) or cream, some bartenders recommend an initial dry shake, which means without ice. The purpose of this is to aerate the liquid at a higher temperature, thus producing a creamy, foamy drink. After an initial dry shake for 7–10 seconds, add ice and shake traditionally.

21

Throwing
This old European style is an increasingly popular technique in bars. Throwing refers to mixing a cocktail by pouring the ingredients back and forth from shaker to glass, to aerate the drink and chill it. Four or five times should be enough. Make sure you use a Hawthorn strainer to keep the ice in the shaker.

Stirring
The purpose of stirring a cocktail is to combine ingredients gently and to chill it, without causing a rumpus in the receptacle. The key is to stir smoothly and gently – you don't want to add bubbles – for 20–30 seconds using a long spoon that can reach to the bottom of the mixing glass. If you want to lower the temperature, keep stirring for a minute and a half.

Swizzling
Putting a clever spin on stirring, the swizzle originated in the Caribbean. Put a bar spoon or a swizzle stick in the drink, and spin the spoon or swizzle stick between the palms of your hands, as if you are trying to warm up your hands. It will mix the liquids and cool the drink – and it looks a little more interesting than stirring.

Straining
The straining technique is mentioned in the equipment section, but some drinks require a double straining using a fine sieve, such as a tea strainer (22). This removes from a shaken cocktail even more ice shards that might affect the flavour.

Muddling
This is a technique for mashing fruit to extract the juice (and oil from the skins) or for mixing fruit with sugar. Simply press the fruit into the base of a strong glass. Although most commonly used for lemon, lime or orange, it can also be used with berries. However, for very soft fruits such as raspberries and ripe strawberries, shaking is usually enough.

Adding a twist
The best way to make a lemon or orange twist is with a potato peeler. Use just like you would on a potato for an easy, efficient twist.

Zesting
For this you scrape yourself a slice of peel, using a potato peeler as above, but here you don't really want the zest. Instead, holding it over the drink, give it a twist to break the surface, releasing the oils and aroma from the peel into the drink.

Building
The technique for building a cocktail is fairly simple. The key is to add the ingredients to the glass it is to be served in over ice, but specifically in the order suggested by the mixologist.

22

INGREDIENTS

As with cooking, you should always use the best, freshest ingredients you can when making cocktails. Attention to detail, whether that be the spirit you use or the ice you serve, is key.

Fruit and fruit juice

Always use fresh fruit. Make it organic if you can, and obviously lemons and limes must be unwaxed. The flavour of fruit changes through the year as it ripens, so make sure you taste the fruit and amend the quantities accordingly.

Ice

Forget about buying ice or making your own using tap water – instead, make your own ice from boiled water. Fill an empty ice-cream container with boiled spring water and freeze it, then take it out of the freezer and use an ice pick (24) or a thoroughly cleaned screwdriver to chip it into large blocks. This will give you the purest and best-tasting ice cubes you can make at home.

To crush ice, if you don't have an ice-crushing appliance, fill a freezer bag with ice. Bash it carefully with a rolling pin until it is sufficiently crushed. Hand-carved ice (23) is, as the name suggests, literally a block of ice fashioned into a more pleasing shape (usually round) using a knife or grater (depending on how confident you are). It is usually best to hold the block of ice in a tea towel making it easier to hold while you carve and reduce the speed at which it melts.

Sugar syrup

Many cocktails require a sugar syrup, sometimes called gomme syrup. This is simple to make by combining one part sugar to one part warm water – the water should be warm enough that all the sugar dissolves. Once the sugar has dissolved, decant to a bottle and refrigerate. For a thinner, less sweet syrup, use a ratio of two parts water to one part sugar. You can also flavour your syrup with herbs and fruit for an added twist.

Infusions

Fruit-infused spirits such as gin or vodka are popular and versatile. The technique for flavouring a base spirit with fruit, spice, herbs or tea is fairly straightforward, is definitely worth trying and is explained within the recipes in this book.

21

23

24

Appendix

COCKTAIL CREATIONS BY

Ladislav Piljar from
The Red Bar at Bam-Bou
1 Percy Street
London W1T 1DB
T 020 7323 9130
bam-bou.co.uk/the-red-bar-
cocktails

Gareth Evans from
*Blind Pig at The Social
Eating House*
58 Poland Street
London WF 7NR
T 020 7993 3251
socialeatinghouse.com

Milos Popovic from
Old Bengal Bar
16 New Street
London EC2M 4TR
T 020 3503 0780
oldbengalbar.co.uk

Francesco Turro Turrini from
Lanes Of London
140 Park Lane
London W1K 7AA
T 020 7647 5664
lanesoflondon.co.uk

Scott Green from
34
34 Grosvenor Square
(Entrance on South Audley
Street), London W1K 2HD
T 020 3350 3434
34-restaurant.co.uk/cocktails

Dino Koletsas from
Rev J W Simpson
32 Goodge Street
London W1T 2QJ
T 020 3174 1155
revjwsimpson.com

Agostino Perrone from
*The Connaught Bar at
The Connaught Hotel*
Carlos Place
London W1K 2AL
T 020 7314 3419
the-connaught.co.uk/mayfair-
bars/connaught-bar/

Thomas Aske from
*The Worship Street
Whistling Shop*
63 Worship Street
London EC2A 2DU
T 020 7247 0015
whistlingshop.com

Simone Caporale from
Artesian Bar at The Langham
1C Portland Place
London W1B 1JA
T 020 7636 1000
artesian-bar.co.uk

Ryan Chetiyawardana from
White Lyan
153–155 Hoxton Street
London N1 6PJ
T 020 3011 1153
whitelyan.com

And finally...

The Maestro
Salvatore Calabrese from
*Salvatore's Bar at the
Playboy Club*
14 Old Park Lane
London W1K 1ND
T 020 3582 6641
playboyclublondon.com/club/
salvatores-bar

ALL GLASSWARE AVAILABLE FROM JOHN LEWIS

John Lewis
300 Oxford Street
London W1A 1EX
T 0844 693 1765
johnlewis.com

ALL COCKTAIL KIT FEATURED, COURTESY OF ALESSI

Alessi Flagship Store
22 Brook Street
London W1K 5DF
T 020 7518 9091
alessi.com

Index

An Hachette UK Company
www.hachette.co.uk

First published in Great Britain
in 2014 by Mitchell Beazley,
a division of Octopus Publishing
Group Ltd
Endeavour House,
189 Shaftesbury Avenue,
London WC2H 8JY
www.octopusbooks.co.uk
www.octopusbooksusa.com

Distributed in the US by
Hachette Book Group USA
237 Park Avenue
New York NY 10017 USA

Distributed in Canada by
Canadian Manda Group
664 Annette Street, Toronto,
Ontario, Canada M6S 2C8

A CIP catalogue record for
this book is available from the
British Library.

ISBN 978 1 84533 952 4
Printed and bound in China

Editor Paul Henderson
Publisher Denise Bates
Senior Editor Sybella Stephens
Photography Romas Foord
Photographic Director
Georgina Breitmeyer
Senior Art Editor
Juliette Norsworthy
Design Untitled
Assistant Production Manager
Caroline Alberti

Contributors
Dominic Bliss
Jennifer Bradly
Ian Cameron
Louise Donovan
Alex Godfrey
Amy Matthews
John Naughton

Thanks to everyone at *GQ*
Dylan Jones
Bill Prince
Mark Russell
Harriet Wilson

Special thanks to
Julian Alexander
Alvin Caudwell
(Caprice Holdings)
Natalie Dunbar
(Sauce Communications)
Paula Fitzherbert & Benjamin
Spriggs (Maybourne Hotel
Group)
Clare Gillespie (Luchford APM)
Alexander Irving (Bacchus PR)
Anne Kapranos (Kapranos PR)